Conscious Curiosity:
Communicating to Connect.

Conscious Curiosity: Communicating to Connect.
Copyright © 2015 Suzanne Gibbs

This title will also be available as an e-book. Visit www.suzannegibbs.com for further information.

Published By: Suzanne Gibbs Studio, Tustin, California

All rights reserved. No part of this book may be stored, copied, or reproduced without prior permission of the author and publisher: Suzanne Gibbs. Requests for information should be addressed to Suzanne Gibbs, 270 S Prospect Ave, Unit A, Tustin, CA 92780.

ISBN-13: 978-0692340875 (Suzanne Gibbs)
ISBN-10: 0692340874

1. Curiosity
2. Relationship
3. Couples
4. Partnership
5. Commitment
6. Communication
7. Conversation
8. Collaboration
9. Talking
10. Listening
11. Self-help
12. Cash
13. Transitions in life
14. Changing Roles
15. Creating Dreams

All quotes are referenced to their authors throughout the book. These quotes are intended as inspiration and as a resource to further study on the topics discussed. They are not intended as endorsement, nor have the authors approved this authors' use of the quotes herein.

Cover Design, Interior Design, Layout, and Illustrations: Suzanne Gibbs

Print copies for personal use only.
First Published in the United States of America, 2015

Note to reader.

*Conscious Curiosity: Communicating to Connect* is a book for contemporary couples that are serious about reaching new levels of understanding in their relationship through the art of conversation. The content is designed to help couples develop intimate communication and collaboration skills through the process of asking questions. Not simply a few questions, but hundreds of questions. The questions are outlined in a manner to help initiate conversations for pressing issues as well as ordinary daily stuff. Continued use of the skills offered in this book will help couples sustain listening, daily talking, information sharing, dreaming about a better future together, deeper understanding, and increasing the feeling of intimacy within their relationship. Basically I am promising you a better life! Are you ready to use a tool called: conscious curiosity? Are you ready to create conversation and connection with your life partner?

This book was originally titled SMD_LMP*. At the ninth hour, and about two weeks before my planned publication date, I changed my mind. I changed the title. I changed how I wanted to reach my audience. That's when Conscious Curiosity was born. I developed the acronym SMD_LMP as a reminder of the intensity needed to sustain intimate, long lasting, and vibrant communication between two people. Unfortunately, the words themselves that made up the acronym could be found as wholly

---

* SMD_LMP is an acronym. In this book, I will make a comparison of the physical intensity of the private intimate act of oral sex to the emotional intimacy of the private intimate act of excellent communication and conversation between two consenting adults. For more information on the meaning of SMD_LMP and the original story behind the proposed use of the acronym, please refer to the sections titled: Mealtime At Our House and Authors Notes.

offensive to too many people. I am aware that history shows us that what was once offensive; may later prove to be inoffensive, but I was not ready for the challenge of making others feel uncomfortable.

Since I had written this book to help couples find a path towards a gentler and kinder relationship; and ultimately allowing their love to reach out into humanity, I felt that I needed to reach out with my own kindness and compassion, not foul language or slang acronyms.

Also, I knew I would not be able to reach as many people as I would like if they could not see beyond the title. Ironically, I ditched the title even though I will be asking you to ditch what you think you know about your partner. I want you to delve deeper in knowledge of each other than you ever thought possible. This book is a tool that can be used to move towards better understanding and communication.

> *True intimacy comes when we give up our own story and let another's heart be truly heard.* — Leonie Dawson

I know that remaining consciously curious in my daily life has brought me much joy and knowledge in my relationship with my husband, children, family, friends, and others. I think about the state of marriages — and divorce. I think about why? I think about the cost of the pain of divorce on children, all people involved, and society at large.

The landscape of modern marriage is shifting. In writing this book my intent is to try to set out some ideas of how to navigate the expanding role of men and women in today's faster pace and highly public social atmosphere. The technology we use today creates altered patterns of communication between two people. Where once plans needed to be made well in advance and adhered to in order to meet up with one another, today people rely on up to the minute texts (or social media platforms) to create face-to-face encounters. Where once upon a time private family matters remained relatively private, today, every surgery, home remodel, job loss and more is shared on social networking sites. Your personal business goes well beyond your immediate family, neighborhood, and community. Today, personal life choices are often in the realm of being visible and known to *everyone* on the whole planet.

Technology can either help or hinder partnerships, families, and friendships. If not handled with care, the latter will be more likely. I love technology, the use of personal computing allowed me to write, draw, design, edit, and publish this book with little outside help. However, I would not have had any ideas to share if I had not made the effort to create daily conscious face-to-face conversations.

Many of us, myself included, cannot imagine a time without our smart phones. We rely heavily on the information found in the palm of our hands to live our daily life. I am curious as to the long-term effects of communicating without face-to-face conversations. I am so curious in fact, that I decided to devote a year to writing about creating more face-to-face conversations with my husband. And I am sharing what I have begun to learn in this book.

Let's wake up to the potential of changing the world through consciously curious questioning, listening, and sharing through communication designed to help people connect on a deeper level and importantly face-to-face.

*For Anna Jones. Live life fully each day. 2009 – 2014.*

Suzanne Gibbs

Conscious Curiosity: Communicating to Connect. i
Introduction: My Story, ahem...Our Story 17
   Power of Talking and Listening 17
   A Little Bit About Me 19
   A Few Notes of Warning 20
   Passion, Mission, Vision 30
   An Introduction According to My Mother 32
   Notes About Cash 33
   Gosh, One More Note 34

Chapter 1 — Hard Work That Never Ends 37
   Hard Work 37
   Dreaming Together 41
   Looking Inside 46
   Coming Out 56

Chapter 2 — Listening: Hint, Less Talking! 59
   Listening is More Critical Than Talking 59
   Not Talking 62
   Active Listening 66
   Ears 68
   Shared Listening 69
   Me Statements 72
   Last Little Bit About Listening 74

Chapter 3 — All Kinds Of Married 77
   Definitions 77

Chapter 4 — Truth: Bring Out the Best 85
   Truth List 86
   Looking for Truth 88
   Time, Resources, Boundaries 90
   Relationship Playdate 92
   Leadership 95

Chapter 5 — Trophy Relationship or Real Relationship 99

| | |
|---|---|
| Saying It Is Not Living It | 99 |
| What Kind of Couple Do We Want to Be? | 102 |
| Conversation Starter Questions | 103 |
| Relationship Intersections | 111 |
| Care and Feeding | 114 |

## Chapter 6 — Mastermind Planning  117

| | |
|---|---|
| The Treasure Hunt | 117 |
| Change Is Inevitable | 120 |
| Hints and Tips | 123 |
| Financial | 123 |
| Health | 128 |
| Work | 142 |
| Home | 144 |
| Cars | 147 |
| Travel | 148 |
| Education | 150 |
| Entertainment | 152 |
| Sex | 154 |
| Kids | 158 |
| Spiritual/Religion/Philosophy | 162 |
| Politics and Activism | 165 |
| Philanthropy | 168 |
| Birthdays, Celebrations, and Other Big Events | 170 |
| Chores | 171 |
| Family Care and Elder Care | 174 |
| Friends | 176 |
| Clothing | 180 |
| Hobbies | 182 |
| Pets and Animals | 184 |
| Volunteer | 185 |
| Time | 188 |
| Mastermind Mentors | 190 |
| Robbing A Bank | 190 |

## Chapter 7 — Fill In the Numbers 193
Cash 193
Chart Your Cash 196
Chart Your Future 199

## Chapter 8 — Non-Verbal Communication 205
Touch the Ones You Love 205
Hearing Is Not Everything 206
Use All Your Body Parts to Talk 208
Love Letters 211
The Technology Equation 214

## Chapter 9 — Blame Games: He Said She Said 225
Play the Game 225
Willing 230
Non-Communication 231
Interrupting 232
Warning Signs 233

## Chapter 10 — Other Uses of Conversation 237
Saving Face 237
Apologizing 239
Forgiveness 240
Promises 241
Accepting and Giving Compliments 242
Negotiating 244
Strategizing 245
Terms of Endearment 246
Report vs. Rapport 246
Confusing Speech 248
Conflict 249

## Chapter 11 — Passion, Mission, and Vision 251
Create Your Own Blueprint 251

## Chapter 12 — Continue the Journey 253
What is in Your Love Box? 253

| | |
|---|---|
| What More Can You Add? | 255 |
| What Needs to be Removed? | 256 |
| Plan to Celebrate | 258 |
| From My Heart to Yours | 262 |

## Chapter 13 — Meal Times at Our House  271
| | |
|---|---|
| How SMD_LMP Came About | 271 |
| A Golden Wedding Anniversary In Our Family | 276 |
| A Bigger Dinner Table | 280 |

## Author's Notes  283
| | |
|---|---|
| About the Original Title | 283 |
| plmk | 288 |

## Acknowledgements  289

## Resources List  293

*I do my thing and you do your thing.*
*I am not in this world to live up to your expectations,*
*And you are not in this world to live up to mine.*
*You are you, and I am I, and if by chance we find each other,*
*it's beautiful. If not, it can't be helped.*

— *Frederick Salomon Perls, Gestalt Therapy Verbatim*

## Introduction: My Story, ahem...Our Story

*Happily ever after is not a fairy tale. It's a choice.*
— Fawn Weaver

### Power of Talking and Listening

I believe in the awesome power of talking and listening. Long lasting relationships need sustained, lasting, and loving communication. Unfortunately, good communication does not come as naturally as we might like it to. We learn communication skills and strategies from those we grew up with, from family, friends, teachers, media, and more. None of this is enough. To be an excellent communicator is a choice. To connect on an intimate level is a choice to be better, get better, learn more, try harder, and most of all to be compassionate, patient, and consciously curious.

The good stuff in life, including communication, requires endless hours of continued practice. I propose that we think about communication in the same ways that we think of other systems and mechanics. Our bodies have countless systems that utilize energy in the form of food to offer us a chance to operate efficiently through out the day. A car engine has many parts that make up the whole to propel us forward on the highway or in our driveway.

In communication, there are countless skills and methods for talking and listening. Mastering even a few of these skills can greatly enhance our ability to harmoniously live with the people we come into contact with on a daily basis. More importantly, excellent communication can strengthen our relationship with our life partner. However, our communication strategies and methods need regular check-ups, the same as we do for our body or our car.

I mean it, when is the last time you checked in with yourself and your partner and asked, "How is the health of our communication?" I bet never! When is the last time you asked each other, "How are we doing on better understanding each other and our future needs?" How are we doing at gratitude and kindness? Do we really "get" one another or not?

> Life must be lived and curiosity kept alive. One must never, for whatever reason, turn his back on life. — Eleanor Roosevelt

My husband regularly asks me this question: "How am I doing?" I always laugh – then I say, "Can you please be more specific?" I admire that he is checking in, yet I am never sure exactly what kind of feedback he is seeking. This is however, a great question. He is initiating a way for us to engage and verbally check-in with one another, by starting with a question. He is starting by being consciously curious.

I am here to tell you that building sustained communication in a committed relationship requires regular check-ups and check-ins. Like going to the doctor for your yearly physical or changing the oil in your car. **Doing a diagnostic on the condition of the communication in your relationship needs to be done regularly or things will go wrong.**

This book is about being curious about your partner. Through asking questions you will find that you are skill building, listening, and finding laughter by conversing. Through conversations I believe deeper communication and trust can develop. Communication is similar to other maintenance routines. For example, testing your blood for ill health or checking the fluid levels during an engine diagnostics. Once you do the tests (for example, ask questions and converse) you can then develop rapport, create new meaning, or create plans for action. Your plan of action will either be to add great new things into your life or to heal areas in need of improvement or repair. In many cases, you may decide to drop what is *not* working.

> Research shows that your best shot at happiness is to make yourself a better partner. — Francine Russo

At the risk of sounding lofty and idealistic, I believe that we can heal the world through deep and committed communication. Things that are broken cannot be fixed unless we address them head-on. Why not start in the home, and the communication between two loving individuals? You did partner up because you love each other, right? Great!

Now, why not check-in, heal, and grow with the support of the person you share your life with? Sounds great, however, intimate conversation is really hard work. Sometimes communicating deeply does not feel like mushy lovely love. Remember to take what you learn from this book and go easy on each other, but don't give up!

Starting the conversations presented on these pages takes courage. Please decide to commit to *starting* conversations. Then, sustaining conversations with your partner will be a lifetime practice.

I believe there is strength in the power of commitment, communication, and collaboration. Sustained loving conversations that begin between two loving people can grow out into the world and enrich the lives of many. However, the conversation needs to start with you and a commitment to be the best person possible.

## A Little Bit About Me

I am consciously creating new adventures and new things in my life — all of the time. I have worked in many different types of organizations from educational institutions, to Fortune 500 corporations, tech start-ups, small businesses, non-profits, and most often, self-employment. I have remodeled homes, been a landlord, taught art, made art, crafted greeting cards and anything else that needed crafting like costumes, projects, and home décor items.

I have traveled and lived in dozens of new places, including abroad. I am married and we are raising two children. I have returned to school twice for two different masters degrees and several other times for continued education. I have close friendships and family scattered throughout the United States. I exist in a comfortable, settled, stable, and committed relationship.

None of this happened by chance. I plan. I build. I study. Mostly, I work hard at creating the life I wish to live.

*I believe you can too.*

My creative soul thrives on making the stuff that is in my head and heart become a reality. This book is one such project. I thank my husband here and in public for being the person that brings home the steady and reliable paycheck. He's awesome that way (and in many other ways too)! I, to quote my mother in law, am a visionary, "Honey, you see things and make them happen! And...I always wonder... what's next?" The what's next has been this book, it has taken me over a year to write and research. I am thrilled to share it with you!

## A Few Notes of Warning

This book presents my opinions. I'd like to mention up front, that I appear on the outside to be a "conservative," you know the kind: white girl, married to white man, stay-at-home momma type, a slew of college years behind me, and a Catholic upbringing. I am, to coin a slang term I learned from a family member – White Bread – but please do not hold this against me! Nor should you think that this image tells the whole story. We seldom fully know the people we think we know.

By becoming consciously curious, first impressions of other people will almost always change.

Sliced white bread.

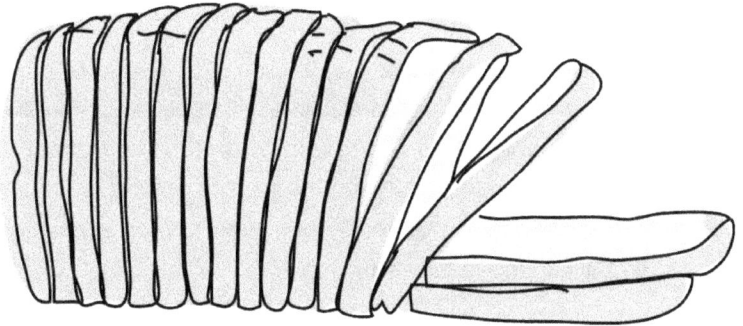

On the inside I am insatiably curious. I am constantly questioning the status quo. I am consciously trying to learn to see as many sides of societal problems and challenges as possible. I am not comfortable with the way many human issues and rights are not moving fast enough towards positive outcomes for all. I am not comfortable about how we treat women or men, our environment, our children, and employees in many corporations and places of business. We have at our fingertips — or better said, our conversation lips — tremendous room for opportunity and growth as humans.

Those who have met me would likely tell you that I am not afraid to ask questions when I am curious about something. When my naïve and playful mind wants to know something, I ask questions.

I do not understand why the world works the way it does. I do understand that things could be better for many people. In my opinion, our so-called "laws" are not protective. There are deeper moral issues and ideals that can be strived for, that need to be sought out. The higher goals can only be reached through:

1. Communication
2. Face-to-face human interaction
3. Touch
4. Trust

Our most humane leaders all used these tools and you can choose to lead yourself to be a humane and loving person as well. I am asking you to start with the person you have chosen as your life partner. Be curious. Ask them what makes them thrive, feel alive, and feel loved.

> *I believe clear, honest, and curious communication is a terrific system for getting to know one another on a personal level. Using compassion and patience while listening, is a path to healing the problems in our world.*

A modern day self published book can be used similarly to a soapbox speech of years gone by. So, instead of a talking in a public space in person, I wrote a book. Obviously, I have a few opinions that I'd like to share. Before we even get started on conscious curiosity for communication, allow me to expound upon a few current-day issues that I think could use our leadership, time, and talent.

All people deserve an education, most especially, literacy. I hate guns and the right to bear arms in America (there was a place for this right at one time, however we live so much more densely now that this law no longer holds all people in high regard). The so-called War On Drugs is stupid and will never work. The entire economy of the United States now depends on illegal drug usage, sales, and the ensuing law enforcement remedies; and this pisses me off! All money exchanged at every level of politics should be outlawed. Our forefathers intended for the government to be by the people for the people and the money in political agendas ruins any possibility of a true democracy in the way our forefathers tried to imagine.

The food industry and the government guidelines for health in America are killing us faster than the guns that I hate. Poverty in America is a disgrace to our nation. Homeless children are an even bigger disgrace. The debt limit is a huge hunk of shit; we should all do a better job of limiting and eliminating our own personal debt. By starting at home, we can teach our government about what we truly value. If we set the example, then maybe our government could learn from us, especially since we are the government — for the people, by the people and all that. My personal goal, however naïve this may be, is to live debt free!

> *The key to eternal happiness is low overhead and no debt.*
> *— Lynda Barry*

All religious leaders should begin to realize that peace, love, and acceptance is much more important than dogma. Ok, I am stepping off my soapbox, that's enough for now, thanks for reading!

My husband frequently says to me in the middle of one of my soapbox soliloquies, "Well, why don't you do something about it!?!" I have not known were to start, until now. I decided to start with myself. I wondered if I could change myself to be a person I can be proud of. I decided to be curious about what I could do to make the world a better place. I asked myself, "How can I be a better communicator? How can I be the change I want to see?" This book is a beginning. I have made tremendous personal changes over the past three years, and I have more to aspire to in the coming years. I am choosing to put myself out there with Conscious Curiosity!

BUT, I have some warnings for you.

**Warning Number 1:**
The curiosity and desire must begin with you.

This book is about relationships and sustained, loving, opening, growing, challenging, and beautiful communication. All kinds of relationships can be serviced with the tools in this book. New ones. Old ones. Used ones. And even ones on rocky footing. This book is about communication and collaboration, there will even be some discussion of cash, if you choose to embark on the chapters Mastermind Planning (Chapter 6) and Fill In The Numbers (Chapter 7).

This book focuses on building the skills of talking and listening – but mostly of sharing of yourself and your dreams for a stronger relationship and better life with your partner. I believe in the potential for change and growth through sharing your time using words, ideas, and images.

> *I believe in taking personal responsibility.*
> *I believe in maintaining an eager willingness to learn.*
> *I believe in conscious curiosity.*

In this book, I share what has helped me to build deeper conversations with my husband and family. I share lists of stuff to try. *If you want to see BIG change* you will need to make a commitment to doing the work in this book. If you picked up Conscious Curiosity to initiate change in your relationship, then DO the work, please. However, feel free to wander through the book and explore the offerings if that's how you'd rather float. I think you'll still get something from this gift I bring to you, and it bears repeating, much more wonderfulness will come through *doing* the work.

This is your book. The time you spend with the content is time you do not spend doing something else. I am extraordinarily grateful that you are spending time with my ideas and opinions as presented. Thank you. Together, with curiosity and communication we can begin to heal the world and humanity. To use the book, you are using your private time. I honor this gift you are giving to yourself, each other, and by extension the world. The content is for you to use exactly as you please. I know and believe you'll do what is best for yourself and your relationship.

**Warning Number 2:**
This book can get addictive. You will find that it is *fun* to connect on a deeper level with your partner through a genuine desire to learn more and by talking and listening to one another. You may even find that the intimacy you find with your partner will spill over into the relationships you have with all those around you (I hope so!).

**Warning Number 3:**
Yes, you can get burnt out on talking and listening to each other and that's no fun at all. Remember to put down the book and do something else, something fun and different, once in a while. Go outside and get active or rest through meditation and self-care.

**Warning Number 4:**
I am an intense planner and I get upset when things do not go as planned. I wrote the book as a way to introduce my own planning (or shall I say dreaming) methods, yikes! Yes, I really did. They may not work for you, please take from this book what does work for you. Honestly, there might be more planning as a result of this book than is truly necessary, or maybe not.

You see, I believe that individuals, organizations, families, and couples need a blueprint to live by in order to reach best possible outcomes. This book, if the work is done in its entirety, can help you to build your relationship blueprint and uncover your passion, mission and vision. You can also fill your love box, to read more on that go to Chapter 12, Continue the Journey.

Throughout my life, I have created my own personal blueprint by developing and writing down my ideas and plans and refining my passion, mission, and vision for life. I did this through asking myself millions of questions and answering them, in writing. I have done this repeatedly, throughout my life.

I am a journal keeper and a question asker. You may not be, but I can tell you from experience that writing can help you plan and can help you to not repeat the same mistakes. For many people writing is an excellent tool for self-reflection. Having ideas dancing around in your head is not the same as writing down your ideas and acting on them.

Keep in mind, even with expert planning life still has a way of ebbing and flowing in unexpected directions. You will need to embrace this reality of life. You will need to pick up, and move on as needed.

**Warning Number 5:**
I am not the expert.

I do not have a psychology degree, or any sort of counseling or expert education on relationships. This is not a PhD mumbo jumbo marriage-counseling book (you likely already figured that out).

What I *have* done is this: I have made a book that began as a way for me to ask myself, "So, where do I go from here?" The result of my curiosity is that the content of the book and doing the work to develop the content has helped my husband and I find deeper knowledge about what we want as a couple. Well, honestly, I found more of ME first, then more about us as a couple.

For those of you who prefer to learn from people with credentials, I have some. I have practiced making art and creating from what is inside me for most of my life. In having completed two master's degrees (one in communication the other in fine art), I have learned a bit about looking for questions, researching my hypothesis, stating my opinion, creating from my innermost beliefs, and reaching conclusions. As a creative individual, I constantly feel compelled to share my thoughts and ideas, via my art and my writing.

> *Would you rather be right, or would you rather be happy?*
> *— Tom Magliozzi*

Compiled in this book are many of the questions I have asked myself and my husband. Now you can use the words and questions in this book as a guide. While you are reading and asking and listening and talking you might find yourselves wanting to begin to think about developing your passion, mission, and vision for life. This is the bigger work, and is not necessary for deeper connection to develop in your relationship. However, getting to your passion, mission, and vision for life as a couple could make your life sparkle with amazing stories and lasting memories. Having a stated passion, mission, and vision can also put your relationship in a place to affect positive change in the world around you.

I am not an expert, but I have expertly tried to do my best to be of service to you.

**Warning Number 6:**
I am a girl. I talk like a girl. I do things like a girl. I like to play and draw and write from the heart. Some of the suggestions in this book may seem down right ridiculous to men and even to many women. I am a girl, yet I cannot possibly speak for all women and make a book that resonates with all people. I have been a woman trying to do what is best and right and expected of me for so very long. In this book, a part of my journey was to be curious about what I could do that is *not* expected of me. I gave myself a book to share the best of me. I am a girl and I

love to talk! Conscious Curiosity serves as a forum to share my ideas, some are good some may be awful. I warned you!

**Warning Number 7:**

I have more questions for you than answers. If I am brutally honest with myself, I still have so many more questions for myself and for my life! Even after writing and examining all of the ideas in this book!

I think if we run out of ideas and interests to explore, life would indeed be quite stagnant and sad. Questions come from curiosity and curiosity is beautiful.

**Warning Number 8:**

I am an impractical, sensitive, and intuitive dreamer.

If you do not believe in following your dreams, you might have picked up the wrong book.

Believe in dreams!

Consider this, do you believe in the possibility of wonderful and impractical dreams being turned into reality? Do you dare to follow your passion, mission, and vision for life as a person and as a couple to create a relationship where abundance thrives? Yes, including cash abundance! Well, then ignore the warnings and jump right in. I hope that what I wrote can help you to connect to your own stories.

**Warning Number 9:**

Curiosity killed the cat.

But, satisfaction brought it back. I won't be satisfied until I see more people living a beautiful, peaceful, and healthy life. I am consciously curious and well, I am asking you to be as well!

## Passion, Mission, Vision

I have a personal passion, mission, and vision. The words tend to alter and shift from time to time, but for today I will share my current passion, mission, and vision.

**My Passion** is to keep my own creative soul alive; she is endlessly delicate and seriously strong.

**My Mission** is to help others find, wake up, or tend to their best creative life. I do this though making art, working on art with others, writing, and encouraging conversation. Through my continued interest in creative pursuits, I share beauty, peace, and health.

**My Vision** is for the world to be the kind and gentle world I that I vividly see in my imagination. Death, ill will, misunderstanding, and destruction are a part of life, I know this, but I intend to dwell on the kind and gentle moments, as well as love, sharing, gratitude, and peace. Communication, be it visual or through words are my tools.

*I am here, writing, to serve you.*

Conscious Curiosity is written to help you to make room for listening, talking, tears, and laughter in your primary relationship. The content is meant for couples to learn how to communicate to connect. This can be accomplished by talking and listening to one another day in and day out. An even bigger beauty comes from a life with passion, mission and vision shared with the person you love.

I was 27 when I married. I did not have enough information to create a viable life-long mission or vision for our union. I do remember having a commitment to try to move towards a shared passion, mission, and vision. When we got married we wrote a statement for our guests in our wedding program. I will share it here with you:

> *We believe that the Lord has brought us together for reasons we will discover as time goes on and days pass. We are here to express our love for one another in front of our families, friends and community to pass on the sacrament and tradition of Holy Matrimony. Thank you for coming here today to share with us on this very special occasion to express our love and commitment to each other for all the days of our lives.*
> *— Derek and Suzanne*

While our statement to our families is beautiful, it is also lacking in detail. The detail is what we have been creating in our life together. Sharing time and conversations with your partner will create the details of your life. You will likely find that talking and listening to one another is of utmost importance.

## An Introduction According to My Mother

Many years ago I gave my mother a chance to tell me what she feels is needed to sustain a committed loving relationship. I was curious and I simply asked her: "What three things do you think are most important to sustaining a marriage?" At the time she had been married about 40 years or so…and without hesitation she gave me an answer. I have pondered her words ever since.

*My mother said that in committed relationships you really only need three things: communication, collaboration and cash.*

Recently, I spoke to my mother about this topic and I asked her if she would add Faith as a fourth element. Without hesitation she said, "Yes." To love deeply and fully trusting your partner takes faith. I say that, to read and try the exercises in a book such as the one you are holding in your hands, you will need to have faith to believe that what is inside the book can make a difference in your life. You will need to have faith that your partner is willing to be honest and give the work and your relationship a solid effort. Faith also comes in forms of religious and spiritual practices in your life. Having faith is not easy to practice, yet it is crucial.

> *My Mom had the idea of the Three C's of Marriage:*
> *Communication*
> *Collaboration*
> *Cash*

PLUS, I have talked to her recently, and we agree, we've added a fourth element: Faith.

I could skip writing this book and share only her wise and commonsense statement of: The Three C's coupled with Faith. She is right that working on communication, collaboration and cash answers the question about how to sustain a relationship.

Still, I wanted to write the whole book. I had a desire to share what has worked for me in sustaining a long-term relationship, and the ideas behind communication, collaboration, cash and faith all needed a bit more fleshing out.

I used all these words and pages to support her common sense. Taking the journey through the work I outline here I was able to support my growth in my own relationship. By extension, from the book in front of you, hopefully your relationship can grow as well. This book is my gift from her, shared with you.

Only after I wrote 40% of the content did I realize I was following and sharing her sage advice! It was as this book took shape, that I remembered her words. Since I am essentially stealing her wisdom, I thought it quite pertinent to give her idea this special Introduction. And most important of all to say, "Thanks, Mom."

In your hands is a whole book of curious ways to start conversations with your partner. Conversations require communication, so that covers: communication. Communication can lead to collaboration and I am quite sure you will find that collaboration will lead to better cash flow. And because life is what it is, you need faith. Have faith in any form that feels appropriate to you. Keep the faith and keep on giving to your relationship. You will be glad you did!

## Notes About Cash

I am not here to tell you how to manage your finances and I cannot create cash flow for you. Only you can do that! I would wager that once you do the work in this book, there is a good chance that your money will be spent on what you value as a couple. Less money will be squandered on unnecessary stuff!

> *Less money spent on stuff that does not support your goals as a couple means you can keep more in savings. Saving over time equals wealth.*

The conversation starters in this book (especially in Chapter 6, Mastermind Planning) can uncover possible cash flow potential. When you both understand what is important to a life well lived together, you can save cash by avoiding unnecessary and unfulfilling tasks, adventures or fill-the-void ventures. Possibly, you will uncover a dream that becomes a business venture.

Please do yourself the favor of hiring professional help (or looking for *free* professional help) if your finances are completely out of whack — meaning you have zero savings and you barely live paycheck-to-paycheck, you deserve a better life, except no one is going to serve it to you on a silver platter or even on a plastic one. Find help. Use help. I wish the best for you financially.

To prove that Conscious Curiosity can create significant shifts in relationships, first, I had to make this book a reality. Second, I had to read and try the pages and work with my husband. Third, I had to put changes into place in my life that aligned with what I have said on these pages.

Before I did *any* of this, I had to look at our own finances and make sure I could devote time to writing and creating instead of earning a living. Having covered my basis (as much as possible), I was ready to write, draw, imagine, and publish. I did what I set out to do and now: Conscious Curiosity is in your hands! And, on that note, let's begin!

## Gosh. One More Note

**How to Use This Book.** Before we begin, I need to tell you that there are many places in this book where I will ask you to take the time to do some thinking, writing, drawing, doodling, and any other note taking activities that work for you. You may want to purchase a notebook and pen to take along while reading or use some sort of note taking program on your computer or tablet.

Better yet, save a bit of money and the planet, and instead search your house for a stack of unused paper and commit to using it for your notes while reading this book. You can make the stack of paper into a bound book by taking it to a print shop and asking for the paper to be trimmed and bound using a coil or comb binding. This small step of taking unused paper from your own home to create a usable notebook will start you on a path of mindful use of your resources.

Now you have this book, you have each other, and repurposed paper for notes. Awesome! I have a huge bias. I believe that taking notes in handwriting is best. You will retain and be able to use more of your own ideas when you see your notes in your own handwriting.

While I wrote I considered how you might use the content in this book. Each time I felt there was an actionable idea, I wrote the words: Take Action. Take action paragraphs are followed by actionable steps. Often in conjunction with the Take Action paragraphs I designed a series of questions or activities and I will ask you to STOP. At these junctures you will see this symbol.

*STOP: Time to take some notes!*

Obviously, you could choose not to take notes, not to share ideas with your partner in writing, and not do the exercises as presented. Obviously, if you choose this route, you will *not* get as much out of this book and the ideas presented. However, it is your time, and your choice.

I believe that writing things down is one of the best ways to untangle and uncover the great ideas living inside of you. I also believe that if you feel compelled to draw or doodle, then please do so! I think people remember stuff better when they figure out ways to make the content visual for their own mind. This will be your choice.

Feel free to use the internet as you fill out the pages in this book. Google searches can assist you in finding details to your dreams with one another and to enhance dialogue. However, also keep in mind that putting away the technology can be beneficial, because *our imagination is immense. Instead of looking for what others other's have done before us, we can tap into what we are deeply called to do and create.*

I have literally hundreds of questions outlined in this book. You may find that you can and do answer all of them. If so, good for you! The notes you take will be especially helpful to you in your journey for use in the last chapter: Continue the Journey. In this chapter you will write, draw, and create a Love Box. Similar in concept to a tool box and specific to your relationship. I am so excited for you, and I hope you are too!

# Chapter 1 —
# Hard Work That Never Ends

*Great sex is hard work.*
*A terrific life is hard work.*
*Intimate conversations are hard work.*
*Work is hard work, and at times...*
*Hard work never ends.*

I send you kisses of love to get you off and running into the hard work of conscious curiosity!

Kisses!

## Hard Work

Ok now, jumping right in! Solid meaningful communication is going to take work, work, work... and I am going to compare this work to: sex. I believe that intimate sexual relations have a lot in common with good face-to-face communication! Seriously, follow me here...

Did you read the story about SMD_LMP yet? No? Well you might want to jump back to the end of the book (Chapter 13, Mealtimes at Our house and Authors Notes, How SMD_LMP Came About), and take a look at the backstory and then return here. I'll still be here, go ahead!

Hey, you're back awesome!

Hearing SMD over and over again for an entire weekend opened an idea in me that created the impetus for writing Conscious Curiosity.

Tug of war.

What I am proposing is that there is a give and take to communication that is similar to performing oral sex. During excellent communication, one person is talking while the other person is actively l-i-s-t-e-n-i-n-g. When performing oral sex, it is possible to share acrobatic positions and perform dual oral sex. However, I wager that the enjoyment for each party is far more likely to happen by allowing one person to concentrate on a singular role within the duality of the act. Sucking dick and licking pussy is not a tug of war, it is an act of love! The hard work of face-to-face communication is in learning to share all of what you have to offer.

Talking and listening, like sex, can be directed to our significant other for his or her benefit and pleasure. Sex is a chance to give of one's self to a partner in a uniquely loving and intimate way. Talking and listening is for the benefit of our relationships as well. Sexual activity must be of loving intent and action for both parties to fully enjoy the experience. My belief is that, like sex, each conversation we have with our partner must communicate with loving intent and action.

*Communicate with loving intent and action.*

And…a bit more about sex! Ask anyone who has been married or in a committed relationship and they will tell you that sometimes you need to have sex even when you don't feel like it! Yea, I know, *nobody* ever wants to talk about this! Usually, in the end, you're glad you did have sex (give to your partner) even when you didn't want to (you do get something in return).

Communication can work very much in the same way. Sometimes you really don't feel like talking or listening, but your partner really needs your empathy and kind regards. Stop what you are doing, even when you don't feel like it, and try to take the time to communicate. You will be glad you did!

If this all sounds like hard work, that's because it is. If this all sounds like giving in, it is not. Developing a committed relationship is about giving as much as taking.

I understand that initiating, growing, and building strong personal relationships is super duper hard work! I am living the hard work of maintaining my long-term relationship with my husband and partner of 22 years. Each day, we learn to give and take what we need from each other. Each day we negotiate our roles within the partnership and practice our version of duality and singularity.

We are committed to strengthening the state or character of being one couple while simultaneously being stronger as individuals and more able to absorb the hardships of life as a whole. Not unlike two-ply toilet paper—stronger and more absorbent.

With this idea of give and take and duality, I wrote. I wrote a lot and I wrote often for several months, many hours each day. I found this work to be hard work worth doing because my larger goal was to help other people to come to deeper appreciation of their significant other.

2-Ply Toilet paper

I smiled each time I embarked on more words to share, more questions for you, and more images to go along with the text. Conscious Curiosity was written one word at a time, similar to how relationships are built with one memory, one hug, one kiss, one touch, and one conversation at a time!

My dream for you is that the practice of wanting to be with one another happens for you like it does for all long term committed partners, one day at a time. I have said it before and I am saying it again: The *hard work* of maintaining a close committed relationship never ends. As anyone knows, hard work needs to be initiated from dreams and passions! Yes?

## Dreaming Together

Before sharing the ideas of Conscious Curiosity with the public, I decided to dream. I used the material in this book with my husband. We are a couple in the stage of marriage that I would call: relationship transitioning. Our children are only at home part-time now. We feel really busy and full of life when they do come home and really empty when they leave go back to school. The empty feeling led us both into a world of looking for stuff to do and stuff to fill our time outside of our marriage.

> *Your curiosity is your growth point. Always.*
> — Danielle LaPorte

We had begun to live each day like roommates do and we were loosing sight of dreaming for our future and loving life as a couple. I imagine that in any given relationship these feelings of being empty, but not forgotten recur from time to time. I imagine that in relationships where both people work outside of the home for most of the day, the roommate feeling could also arise, even without terrific transitions in life. I began to be curious about whether I had some information that might be helpful to other couples.

First, I wanted to know for myself if I could reignite and create a more beautiful future with my spouse. We had so many hopes and dreams when we were young and first engaged to be married. Over the years we had reached some of our dreams, but not all. Somewhere along the line, we began to loose sight of joint dreams. I imagine this happens to all couples from time to time as life ebbs and flows at will!

I knew we needed to reignite our passions for each other through dreaming and reawakening happiness. I had that goal for us! But I knew that neither of us could see inside each other's heart and mind. How could he know I felt like I was a roommate? He couldn't. The time was ripe for me to become curious and trust that we could reignite our connection. I decided we needed conversation starters and intimate communication!

I will be honest. Initially, it was hard to find the time to share and communicate with my own husband. It was a crazy time! Here we were, living life without kids underfoot and still not finding time for each other. I asked for dates. I told him my plans for this book. I begged and cajoled. I asked for even more time together. I used a bit of trickery (asking questions whenever I got his attention). He eventually gave in to my persistence.

> *You cannot teach a man anything; you can only help him to find it within himself. – Galileo*

He relented. At first it was hard to commit to the time it takes to dream together using words, questions, and stories. Our initial conversations started in fits and bursts of energy, and pittled out, or exhausted us. However, we kept trying (after all I had a book to write). Soon, we found ourselves trying to sneak time away from other activities to let the activity of communication grow and nourish us. Then, we would flow toward not communicating once again and we'd pull forward and back into conversations.

I tell you this, because the path towards deeper intimacy with your partner is not a straight path. You will need patience, perseverance, and faith. I guarantee that even though you think you know everything about your partner, you don't.

The stories, exercises, and illustrations in this book are not a cure-all for troubled or even happily committed collaborative relationships. I really do not believe in a cure-all anyway! What there can be is hope. There can be small increments of change. There can be renewed love to the commitment. I gift you the courage to find ways, like we did, of dreaming and laughing together through listening and talking to one another. Investigate the reasons you are a couple. Turn to your natural curiosity about what can be, what possibilities there are, and what more life can offer. Stories coupled with curiosity can lead to more intimate conversation.

With energy focused towards intimate conversation, connection to one another stays or becomes stronger. Intimate conversation also builds trust, an essential element in committed relationships. Our kids still come home from time to time. When they do, we make an effort to have meals together, even when the dinner conversation leads to Sucking Dick (see Chapter 13: Meal Times at Our House) or other unmentionable conversations. In our household, we still find love, humor, and reasons to keep working at our family relationships through conversation. However, intimate deep conversations cannot happen without the commitment to making them happen.

Yes, relationships take work! Relationships require talking and listening ad nauseam! A sense of humor never hurt either! AND GUESS WHAT? THE WORK NEVER ENDS! Yes, I am shouting at you. The hard work of maintaining lasting loving and trusting relationships, NEVER ENDS. Never-ever. But I have already said this haven't I? I am in your face, I think too many people think that they can fix stuff and have a relationship coast merrily along. Honestly, can you think of anything in life that works that way — coasting? Ok, coasting works as coasting, but other stuff does not! Can you fix something and bam, it's all-better? Life is not like that, is it?

> *The flame of a fire needs to be tended to in order to keep burning bright.*

What do I do? I wake up each day choosing to be married to my husband. I choose to be the kind of Mom that will make me proud of myself; I expect my children will grow and learn from their own adventures. I choose to love in the best way I know how. I choose to give of myself to others. I choose to try to turn off my broken inner tapes that no longer serve me or us. I choose to try to learn how to love unconditionally. The continued effort to stay committed to us seems worthwhile, one day at a time, most of the time. I am far from perfect.

How about you? What do you do each day to live in line with your values?

My own relationship to my husband and family is my personal contribution to a better world. I certainly could have made different decisions, ones that may have kept me in line with the expectations that others had for me, or decisions that could have had me in a corporate job, but I did not. Unlike the corporate world, the job of a wife, stay-at-home parent, and artist does not have a measure of success. No regular raises here. No trophies or notoriety for doing the right thing.

I answer to myself.

My motivation is all personal and internal. Sometimes I want a ribbon or a promotion, some outward accolade. Any outside kudos would do — however, whatever might be given to me would pale in comparison to my personal internal motivation for doing the job I do and doing it the best I know how day in and day out.

I call what I do personal responsibility, integrity, and "being an adult." I am a woman, wife, mother, a member of a larger family and community, and I am an artist — the publication of this book will allow me to say I am a writer. I play other roles as well, but these are my primary roles and they are the ones I work the hardest at.

Why do I tell you all of this, because the contents in this book will require you to use your own personal motivation to get started and to keep you going. No outside person is going to tell you to buck up and do the work — you are responsible for your own growth as a human in your relationship to your partner. Your personal integrity is at stake. Your relationship is at stake. To be an adult means to do the work and have the deeper harder more intimate conversation(s).

> One of the biggest things I've learned in relationship counseling is that I can be super skilled in the art of communication blocking – of effectively stopping conversations that I don't want to have. And that in order to have a deep, intimate relationship, I have to be okay with not being in control of a conversation, and hearing things that might not be comfortable for me. — Leonie Dawson

Sometimes, you may find that doing the work; the deepest work requires you to look inside first. How did you get to where you are today? Certainly, you could make an argument for all of the outside influences that brought you to where you are, but if you are 100% honest with yourself — you brought yourself to where you are today.

## Looking Inside

I took a look inside to get the words of this book onto the page. Sometimes what's inside is quite messy. Many times we do not share our internal messes with others for fear of looking foolish or simply for privacy sake. But how can we teach each other to look *inside* for strength and answers if we do not share a bit of our journey with one another? I believe we all have what we need inside to help us to move forward. All we need to do is learn to look, hear, and listen to our inner most self. To listen inwardly takes faith.

You may call the inner most self — God or god, Jesus or wild shaman, the universe or spiritual energy, soul or inner compass, or any other name you like. You may even decide that a higher power is outside of you to guide you, but in the end it is you, that makes tiny daily choices. I am fairly certain most people do not think of themselves as puppets on an invisible string from an invisible outside source. You know what I am talking about; it's that beautiful powerful wondrous inner you that is all knowing, beautiful, strong, and intuitive.

The story of the evolution of this book is not a tidy picture. Life never is all easy and tidy is it? My hope is that by knowing where I came from to write this book and share it with you, you will better be able to relate to the content and gain valuable insight for yourself.

After graduating with my Master of Fine Art (MFA) in May of 2013, I was utterly exhausted. I had traveled a distance of 140+ miles each day by car to class for two years in Los Angeles traffic. During my tenure at Claremont Graduate University, I did my best to keep up with my mostly younger classmates. I worked on expanding my knowledge of art, making art, writing about art, and deciding why I make art. I did not realize it at the time, but for two years I was learning to justify my personal creative existence.

Some of my family obligations suffered as a result of my attendance in graduate school. I am sad about that, but I was determined to blaze a new path for myself, regardless of the consequences. And I must add, I stepped up to my personal responsibilities as soon as I could, post graduation.

> *Living with integrity means: Not settling for less than what you know you deserve in your relationships. Asking for what you want and need from others. Speaking your truth, even though it might create conflict or tension. Behaving in ways that are in harmony with your personal values. Making choices based on what you believe, and not what others believe.*
> — Barbara De Angelis

Upon completion, I thought I was ready to hit the pavement and sell my art (paintings) to hundreds of people. Yea, ha naïve! To accomplish this goal, I began working on my business skills. Because sales, after all, are business skills and business skills are not at all related to the skills of making art. There are hundreds of excellent programs and books available for individuals to improve their business acumen. I enrolled in some on-line classes, read many books, tried lots of ideas, and then, I began to falter. I was still exhausted, even more so than before, and my art was not selling out of my studio in droves. Oh wonders!

I was now beyond exhausted. And I was now attempting to address some of the still lingering personal and family issues that arose from my two years of intense focus in graduate school.

Typical to who I am, when things got too hard I veered off course! I decided to embark on a new project! Sure, why not, take on *more* activity. I worked on my health. I changed how I eat and what I eat. I got myself outside much more often. Then, in less than one year I lost over 35 pounds! Cleaning up my health led me to cleaning up my studio.

Again using intense focus, I miraculously sold over 100 paintings in one month! How? By charging only a few dollars over shipping and packaging costs! How cool is that? The experience was great, but obviously not sustainable. Lots of hard work and my art business bank account well, it basically stayed the same.

Still, I was super proud that I had taken the initiative and really really put myself out there via the internet. I was shipping art daily around the country for a month, how cool is that!?!! Some pieces even went to Canada!

So, here I was, I had shed unwanted weight and I had moved my beautiful paintings into other people's lives! Yeah! I was on a roll. Next, I gave away any paint supplies that made me feel ill, gave me headaches, or induced troubled breathing.

What was left? What I had left was an emptier studio, and a thinner me. And at about this time I was offered my first solo show. Luckily, I am a prolific painter and creator; I had plenty of work still in my studio! I painted a little extra. I did the show, and the experience was terrific, but zero sales! Aargh...what was the universe calling me to work on? Was I meant to keep working and sharing of my ideas and myself for *free*? Was I doing something wrong? Was there something wrong with me? Was the path of a creative the wrong route to take?

I knew what working for free felt like — I had been a parent volunteer for my children's schools and personal interests for many years! Working for free is the comfortable well-worn path in my life. Working for free is great — I can have tons of flexibility with my time. Working for free is awful too; people ask me "what do you do?" and the answer gets stuck somewhere between shame and self-doubt.

There has to be a better solution. Another idea. The next big thing!

I turned towards curiosity.

What else could I do? I sat. I looked at my walls. They were empty of my work. I was empty, but I kept on journaling and spending time outside. I looked through my old work, what was left of it, and pondered. I read old journals and looked at old sketchbooks. I found old notes about writing a book. All this internal mumbo jumbo and soul searching left me still feeling adrift. During this time I applied to over 40 jobs and only landed two interviews, neither of which offered me work.

Exhaustion. Jobless. Art sales not happening. Self doubt. Family crud to deal with. What more?

Goodness gracious there was more! I realized I also missed spending time with my husband! All this clearing, thinking, and recharging my batteries led me to explore *how* I was spending my precious time. My relationship with my studio time changed.

I began spending more quality time with the people I love, most especially, my husband.

What???

Also, I was trying really hard to listen to a deeper clearer me. I am a creative. I need to express, but with what? How? For who? Most of all, WHY am I a creator? What am I meant to communicate? I had so many questions inside of me! And, no answers.

I continued to look inside.

Through my experiences at school, I had one thing. I had gained confidence that I can take on projects that seemed way larger than possible, and see them through to completion. I knew how to respond to my inner curiosity and listen to her.

> Side note: Did I tell you yet that this all came at mid-life? Five-O. Mid-life special, here we come! From what I gather, this is an age where many women take stock of their life. They take the time to look back on their life and look forward. Eh, so I am not so special, I'm normal!

I began to ask myself, "What project needed to be seen through to completion?" I did not know. I began to calm down and look at "the now" at least once each day — a totally new novelty for me! I worked on: "Being." I began regular meditation, taking quiet time, looking blankly at the sky — is this really allowed to happen? What if others found out that I was out smelling roses, looking at trees waving in a breeze, and picking up snails along my long walks? What if others knew I was *not* making a living, only a life?

> All truly great thoughts are conceived by walking.
> — Friedrich Nietzche

What if others found out that, if I was alone and without a husband, I would not be feeding myself, putting a roof over my head, and clothes on my back...within my current chosen path.

I lived a lie.

I have an artist web site, a regular blog, and a regular newsletter — but I felt like a fraud because I would not be able to afford to keep on this path with no income to support the creativity that I so long to nurture and share.

I lived a lie, because I was not honestly striving to be my best. I veered off course repeatedly. I was lost. I wanted someone else to find me and champion my work. That I knew, was unrealistic, but it was the lie I lived for a time.

I began to wonder, doesn't taking the time to meditate, notice my brain talk, and endless personal loops of despair make me look and seem idle? Who was I to be able to give myself this gift of beautiful dreamy nothingness called, being? I am still taking my time to figure out how to reach the age of 50 in a place of great pride and comfort in my life. I also see myself slipping further and further back into my role as a stay-at-home mom even though the kids are moving away and into college.

One step forward, two steps back? Or am I so darn stuck on the old rut that nothing can change my path? I went back to graduate school to advance to a new life and path for myself. Did it work or was it all a waste?

Inside there was a voice and it said and still says, "Keep going." I feel like, my time to do something big has got to happen, now. Even *now* is not soon enough. I get so incredibly frustrated, because I am not seeing my own evolution. I am not finding the endless hours of quiet time I think I need to create all of the visions I see in my creative imagination. At the same time, the endless loops of feeling undervalued and misunderstood crash like waves upon the shore within my brain, heart, and soul. Still, I write daily. If not now, then when?

Idly, I think, I could do something like plan my birthday party...and my Birthday Cake? Yeah, I dream about pyramids of sugar! LOLs, not really, what a bore! The urge to be bigger to myself has declared itself to me through my writing, not Birthday Cake.

> Whispers came to me. Why not write that book that I was being called to write?

I knew wanted to create growth, beauty, and change in the relationships most precious to me — I wanted to start with myself and my relationship with my husband. I wrote this book as a way to re-connect with myself and with him. Like I said earlier, I wanted to dream with him again like we did when we were younger. I wanted to clarify our goals and laugh together once again. Initially, when the book was in it's infancy and had the original title of SMD_LMP, neither of us could say, "Suck My Dick and Lick My Pussy" without cringing. Yet, soon we were laughing, pulling out the SMD_LMP non-edited beta version of this book to look at it together.

I have to tell you, miracles began to happen. We began connecting on a deeper level. We began to eagerly accept the changes we could see on the horizon in our life together. We do not have a perfect beautiful plan, I still want one, but life unfolds in it's own time.

I trust through continuing to look inside. Through faith.

The book, Conscious Curiosity, is the outcome of writing one word and making one drawing at a time. The future holds a place unknown. There is no room for self-doubt, even though the idea of doubt still lurks in the shadows. I even named my doubt: Jimminy Cricket! He bounces all around me all of the time, surprising me at the most ridiculous times, veering me off path, only to settle right in on my shoulder and shake his head in doubt. He only goes away when I am creating my best life and when I am creating my art or writing. The little bugger!

On the brighter side, healing in our family has begun to happen, and continues. The hard work of looking inside began to show me my way.

*I want this for you. I want even more for you!*

If you're really smart you're thinking right about now, "Is she clueless, doesn't she realize that writing a book is another path to working for *free*?" Yea, ok I know. A creative must do what their heart calls out for them to do — or die inside. Drum-roll please, drama! Dramatics! I'm gonna die if I cannot share my story!

But seriously,

Do yourself a favor.

Look inside. You have all you need to grow, and learn, and thrive. It is all inside of you; all you need to do is be curious and listen. I tell you this story, every personal messy part of it because life is messy. Life takes courage. Life requires that you listen to yourself and be true. I felt that if you could see that you're not alone in your wanderings and confusion and rough spots in life, you could move on by looking inside and listening to yourself. I believe in order to be your best for your partner, you need to know and listen to yourself first!

For me, listening and looking inside ignited my passion — I knew I was supposed to share. Conscious Curiosity is my current gift to each of you and in all honesty, a personal gift even to myself and my own relationship(s).

## Coming Out

Over the past 17 years about 80% of my work has been at home tending to the house and family. Only during two of those years did I dramatically change my focus. These were the two years I spent in graduate school to earn my MFA. I wanted to come out of the home, and I had found no role models to work from, so I went to school. Despite the numbers of books I read on the topic of ramping back into the workforce...I found no work worth leaving the home for...I am not one to give up, instead, I went to school, worked on my creative capacities, I painted like a crazy lady out of jail and I wrote, and wrote, and wrote.

I wrote for me. I wrote blog posts. I wrote endless "Artist Statements." Then, I wrote this book for couples, as a way to come out, and as a way to help others.

I hope I find and learn about how to promote my book! I am in unchartered territory, for me. I want to come out and play in the big world outside of the walls of my home and studio. And while I try on the idea of being a writer I am noticing shifts in the world around me.

I am noticing that the boundaries between what is public and what remains private is rapidly changing. I think the best thing to do is to grow from within, and come out. I try to embrace the changes I feel all around me.

I know I am not the only one to witness half an argument that others are having on a cell phone! I know I am not the only person who has watched an elderly person navigate a grocery store with a phone pressed to his or her ear asking someone at home to once again describe the exact kind of paprika or peanut butter needed! A short time long ago, we would never have witnessed these private moments in public.

I am coming out from being in the home, meanwhile people everywhere are coming out and sharing and baring all through technology and social media. We are all using the current technology to toss ourselves into each other's faces. We put up with other people's conversations even when we wish we did not have to.

Social media forums have pushed and will continue to push the boundaries of what is public verses what remains private in conversations. I have watched the marriages of friends break apart and move into divorce on Facebook. I have been witness to suicides on Facebook. I have been notified of the death of a colleague on Facebook. A very short time ago these events would only become known in face-to-face conversations, or possibly on a phone call! Today, conventions of communication are changing. These changes will continue, but we also need to work like salmon and swim upstream to continue to create the best within our species.

We are people. People talk. People make meaning through conversation. People also create change through conversation. I think it is safe to say that finding happiness comes from moving deeper into conversation. Face-to-face conversation builds trust — and this is not true with video conferencing, teleconferencing, and social media sharing. Touch and eye contact is an element of communication that cannot be overlooked.

Communication will remain intensely important. People thrive through communication — and since talking and listening face-to-face is still the best form of communication, I say, why not start with our primary relationship, the relationship we have with our life long partner.

As far as I can tell, *how* people sustain long-term close committed relationships remains mostly private. There is a great need for developing the skills of stronger private close conversations. I wrote this book to encourage the practice of starting conversations and then continuing to talk and listen. Starting to talk is a beginning, sustaining the conversation creates unbridled intimacy. Please consider starting the work of deepening conversations in private and sharing what you learn publicly.

> *Please, like me, come out and play and become consciously curious.*

Conscious Curiosity is created for use in a manner that is meant to be fun and challenging! Are you ready to come out and converse? I think I am. I have done the hard work of writing this book for you. I am curious, are you ready for the hard work ahead? Will you look in and reach out? Let's not forget to lean on each other and work together to create the world we want to live in. First hard work, then dream big, initiate intimate conversation, look inside, and come out to play. Are you ready? Let's begin with listening!

## Chapter 2 —
## Listening: Hint, Less Talking!

> *The most basic and powerful way to connect to another person is to listen. Just listen. Perhaps the most important thing we ever give each other is our attention.*
> — Rachel Naomi Remen

So, you thought this book was about communication. And you though communication meant talking and being heard. Well, not so fast there! Ideas about talking might have made you think about what you want to say and *have* to say to your partner. Fine. We will get to the act of talking, but not now, later. Please shelf your thoughts and ideas, for now, because, *listening* comes first.

### Listening is More Critical Than Talking

Yes, I will repeat: *Thoughtful listening is more critical than talking* in conversation especially in a committed and sustained relationship. In fact, listening is more important than talking, period. When you think of the word communication, you may first think about what you are saying, what you are planning to say, or what you want to say. For you, communication might be all about getting heard. Unfortunately no, listening is the bigger part of communication. *Listening comes first.* Active listening shows that you care. Listening builds trust. Listening helps build understanding and empathy. In this chapter I will share my favorite listening skills. The first biggie: Not Talking.

Are you familiar with the cash cow matrix in business? You basically have four quadrants that represent the health of different products or services in a business. The quadrants are labeled: Question, Star, Dog, and Cow.

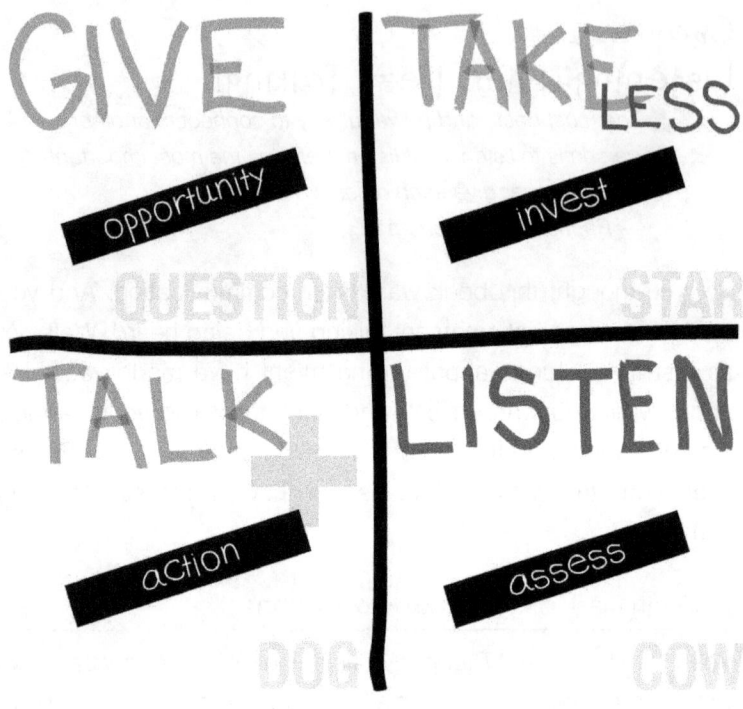

The question quadrant is a place of great opportunity and holds the upper left quadrant. In business, leaders might look to what else can be done and they will look at all angles of a thorny situation. In our matrix the corresponding idea here is to "give." The problem is, sometimes it becomes unnatural to give, and giving sometimes feels like too much! Similar to how business leaders may want to avoid "asking questions." That's the golden opportunity! Give to your loved one even in times when you really don't feel like it! Give by listening, hugs, kisses, and kindness! Look for and create opportunities to give and ask questions! Look at the relationship from as many angles as possible. Where there is a problem or a question, there is *an opportunity to give* your full attention towards reward and resolution.

The Star holds the upper right quadrant, corresponding here to "take." In this matrix, the star represents a period in business were things are going well and appear stable. The advice is to invest more in this quadrant, because things seem to be working! The Star performer is producing, but without further investment, things might go sour. One way to look at this in communication between couples is, if you take too much you will drain your star performer — your partner and yourself. If you don't take enough, your partner will not feel needed! You must invest in your relationship. Invest in time. Invest in energy. Invest in conversations.

The lower left quadrant represents the dog. The dog in business is the product or service that might get cut from the product line, but it once was a vital part of the business. In our matrix this quadrant represents "talk". Sure, talk is good, really good, but it can also be the problem. Do you know what I mean? If all you do is talk with no action, where does that get you? Consider evaluation or liquidation of your habit to talk and not follow through on doing the work you say you'll do. Don't send the dog out into the street! All talk and no action is like a dog barking at the mail delivery person. The mail will keep coming day after day, but the dog has made no noticeable change. If you want to keep the dog, take action.

*Give your partner more than they expect and do it cheerfully.*

The lower right quadrant represents the cow, or in our matrix the need to "listen." The cow is exactly as you'd imagine. The cow represents that product or service in business that seems to do no wrong, it simply makes money, and it certainly makes sense to keep that product or service coming! Listening is the cow of a relationship. I honestly do not think that it is possible to listen too much! Your partner will thank you for being supportive, understanding, and empathetic. However, in business regular "check-ins" and "assessments" are critical to keeping the cow alive. If not, the competition will get ahead and the cow might die. Don't assume you have listened enough, take the time to check-in, assess, and on occasion take a deeper attitude towards listening.

All the quadrants of the matrix work best when they are given equal attention. To build your relationship and to deepen the communication between you and your partner: give, take, talk, and listen with honesty and intent.

## Not Talking

The number one most effective way to listen is to STOP talking. Yikes, too easy right? Well, not so much. I love to talk. I love talking so much that I was labeled "a regular chatterbox" by Sister I-can't-remember-her-name in grade school. Possibly, if I had listened more, I would have remembered her name! Many women love to talk. I have heard it said that women say 20 words to men's every one word during a conversation! This is a generalization that may or may not be true, men sure can chatter on as well. So, ladies and gents out there who love to talk, take heed. STOP talking and start listening.

> *If we were supposed to talk more than we listen, we would have two tongues and one ear. — Mark Twain.*

Conscious Curiosity | 63

Two ears, one mouth!

How can you listen better?

1. Get yourself in a listening frame of mind.
2. Choose to look at the other person in the eye.
3. Choose to focus on the words, feelings, and body language.
4. Turn off your phone, or better yet put it in another room.
5. For that matter, turn off all electronics.
6. Try not talking as much for one day at work…

Take Action. I could list over 20 things that can be done to STOP talking and start listening on a deeper level. Instead, why don't you write down a few ideas of your own? Try writing down 25 ideas! I am guessing that if they are your own, you might listen to them.

> *Special Note: This is the first place to take out your pen and paper and do some writing. Jot down a few ideas on*

*what you can do to improve your own listening skills. Alternately, do some drawing or make a doddle to help you make sense of the information presented.*

A few years ago, I challenged myself to only listen while spending a lovely lunch date with my mother and my aunt. I have no idea why I decided not to talk that day. But I did. And here is what happened. We talked about family, husbands, children, the weather, homes, jobs, and all sorts of topics to catch up on each other's lives. The amazing thing is, I can remember that lunch like it was yesterday, even though it was over 5 years ago! The other amazing thing is, that neither my mother, nor her sister, my aunt, realized I wasn't talking until about two hours into the conversation. I had a marvelous time. What did I do differently? How did I manage to "not talk"? I only responded to direct inquiries. The rest of the time I was focused on listening. I learned more and felt more present in that lunch than when I do "regular" talking and communicating.

Take Action. Here is your challenge. In the next week, pick one conversation with your partner, a family member, or close friend and do a Mark Twain — listen with both ears. This is not meant to be a forever and ever challenge, instead pick any amount of time and try: *not talking*. If not talking works for you like it does for me, then do it more often.

After family gatherings, my husband often asks me, "Why didn't you speak up more during conversations?" Being a listener has allowed me to observe the table dynamics, the conversations, and the relationships. I am sure that they respect my avoidance of conversation in large groups because it makes more time for others to talk. I fear no one even notices, but that does not bother me (at least not most of the time...). Remember how I told you I love to talk? Well, that is only true when I know that others are truly listening. I know myself. I don't need to hear about myself. I am comfortable being an observer in groups and an active listener with individuals. Still, I do love to talk so sometimes I forget my skills and ramble on when I am with my husband or a good friend! That brings us to the next topic: active listening.

## Active Listening

I will never forget the first time I learned about Active Listening. I was in graduate school studying communication; the teacher had us role-play the use of Active Listening Techniques. These techniques are often taught in business settings for people to better hear and understand what the other person has to say. I was excited to go home and try active listening with my husband. We were married less than a year at the time, and I had a blast practicing and learning more about him.

I am guessing he never knew he was an experiment in my studies! Anyway, active listening allowed me to get to know him better. That was a good thing, because we had already lived apart from one another during our first year of marriage. He had joined me in the "new" state we lived in by that time and we certainly wanted to make things work! Through active listening I became a better person and more loving. Writing this has reminded me to work on this skill again, active listening is *not* natural for me. My guess is that active listening is not *natural* for anyone, but like any skill it can be learned.

There are a zillion ways now that instructors use to teach these techniques and skills. A quick Google search and you can get a list of a million or more hits on how to do "active listening" for relationships at work, partners at home, families and more. I want to give you my condensed version. Here is what I remember the most from class 18 years ago:

> After someone has spoken, take the time to paraphrase what he or she said and ask, "Did I hear you correctly?"

Take Action. Can you imagine the huge shifts that would happen if we really listened using active listening? Here are some other phrases you can try.

So, what you are saying is...

What I understand you saying is...

May I repeat back what I heard so that we can make sure I understood you...

Could you try telling me another way so that I can be sure I understand what you are trying to tell me?

Active listening is actively attempting to get the most content, feelings, emotions, and information from the person talking as you possibly can. Active listening is not about trying to hear what you want to hear. Active listening is not about thinking you know what the other person is going to say and therefore ignoring their words. Active listening is learning what the other person is attempting to tell you.

Active listening is the best tool, hands down, for allowing the talker to discover his or her own feelings and emotions. We do not always know where frustration and anger come from, the patterns are often set in childhood, but we can help one another communicate and grow in emotional intelligence.

After you have tried active listening for one or more conversations jot down notes on how it felt, what you learned, and what you need to work on to improve the experience next time.

*STOP: Time to take some notes!*

We use our ears and more for listening, the next section focuses on the power of ears to hear.

## Ears

When I teach children I use all sorts of communication tricks to keep their attention. One of my favorites is to ask them to put on their "deer ears." I use this technique when I have a critical step in teaching an art project and I need them to all get it right and be in the same part of the project at the same time. I show them how to cup their ears with their hands so that they can capture more sound in their eardrums. The act of attempting to capture more sound is invariably going to create an environment for pretending to listen harder. Once they hear the exaggerated sound, the activity becomes a game and a great method to focus their attention.

Take Action. Try making Deer Ears right now for 15 seconds. Take your hands and create cups, then place your thumbs behind your ears snuggly, count 1- 1000, 2- 1000, 3- 1000, until you reach 15. What did you hear that you had not known was a sound that existed before? This is fun yes? Go ahead, put the book down, give this a try!

Deer ears.

Why not? Why not use this simple technique to listen to your partner? What if you tried on your deer ears next time you really want to hear your loved one's words? Yea, you'll look stupid and slightly fishy like if you flap the ears and pretend they are gills...ugh, I digress! Is this catchy? Deer Ears for Active Listening? Make a DEAL with yourself to put on your DEAL's—ha ha. I cannot wait to hear how this challenge works out for my readers!

Keep an important point in mind. Deer can move their ears independently of one another to capture information from different locations at once. Deer often keep track of each other by listening, even when their pack is behind them! They also observe body language to communicate. I have heard people say deer are really stupid animals, but they have an important strength — they *listen* with those big rotating satellite dish sized ears.

Take Action. Pretend you are a deer or some other type of animal with super power hearing for one full conversation. How did you like this form of listening? What went well? What was horrible about the experience? How will you approach listening differently after attempting this exercise?

*STOP: Time to take some notes!*

Ok, so I covered not talking, active listening, and deer ears, I am guessing by now you want your turn to speak! Well, you can. I call the next section shared listening.

## Shared Listening

I learned about the use of a talking stick and how it works in a women's spirit circle that I belonged to over twenty years ago in the mid 1990's. I was and still am, 100% in love with the talking stick method for listening! The talking stick is an easy to use tool for shared listening!

In a nutshell, the person who holds the talking stick gets to be the person who is talking. Everyone else's job is to listen with their ears wide open. The talking stick is a personal favorite because I feel a sense of power when it is my turn to hold the stick and talk. Remember: We all love to be heard! Way back when, I felt wonderful knowing that I was being listened to in a group of women that were my senior! Not only that, hearing some of my words and thoughts reflected back when it was another woman's turn to talk made the experience even more powerful and joyful!

You may be thinking, how juvenile. Aren't talking sticks for kindergarteners (I later learned, after I had children, that many elementary school teachers use talking sticks in their classrooms.). Seriously, you came to this book for ideas, if it seems stupid or juvenile to you then, very likely this is a tool you most need to try. I have found that the ideas that I am most reluctant to try or feel most resistance to are exactly the trick, skill, or knowledge that I really need to get unstuck.

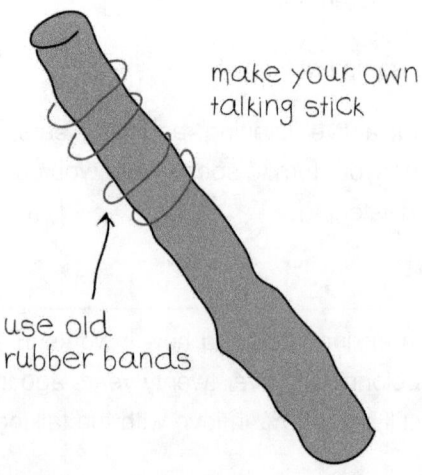

make your own talking stick

use old rubber bands

Take Action. Try using a talking stick — 10 minutes each person, he/she who has the stick can talk, she/he who does not must listen! Simple, 20 minutes and a child can do it! I have seen people hold the talking stick to hold a silent space in conversation — and oh wow, that can be powerful!

Take Action. Need more convincing? Make the adventure of talking stick talking more fun. Take the time with your partner to find the right talking stick. You could go buy a talking stick or rain stick for this purpose. You could make a talking stick together. You could use an existing object in the house that you choose together. In our family we even used a pretzel as a talking stick during a family meeting once, until someone ate it!

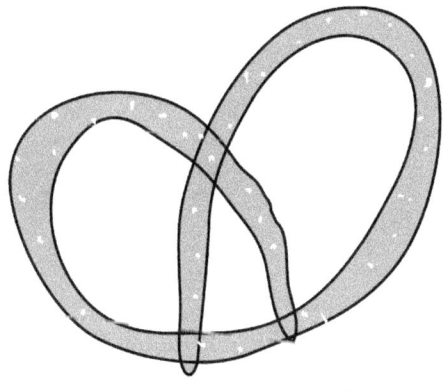

pretzel talking stick

My point is, whether the talking stick is special and expensive, easily available or disposable does not matter one bit. Give the object the power of the talking stick and let the conversation begin. I hope you enjoy being listened to as much as I do! Don't shake a stick at it! Yea, corny I know! Go ahead, try listening to the person with the stick.

Take Action. Use a talking stick for one conversation with your partner or with a child. How did you like the experience? What was awful about handing the stick back and forth? What did you learn from the experience? Did you NOT do a talking stick because the concept seemed too stupid? What can you take from this experience into future conversations? Will you use the talking stick again? If so, for what types of conversations would the use of a talking stick be most suitable?

*STOP: Time to take some notes!*

The talking stick is a great step towards action in our next step — using *me* statements. Me statements may be one of the hardest forms of communication to master. Why? Because you need to be fully in tune with your own feelings and motivations. Ready? Lets move on.

## Me Statements

Me statement are the *opposite* of this:
You this...
You that...
You. You. You.


You statements never work. Instead try using "I," "my" or "me" statements. Me statements are not about listening to the other person. To create really good *me* statements you need to listen deeply to your *own* inner voice. Me statements come from listening to your own feelings. Me statements come from being true and honest with yourself. Me statements are hard work, because you need to let go of your ego, let go of protecting yourself, let go of being right, and dive head first into vulnerability, integrity, and honesty.

I dare you, to try. Me statements might sound like this:

I am going through a confusing time right now, what confuses me is _____

My feelings get all twisted out of shape when I hear you say _____.

When you say _____, I feel _____.

I guess the top three things that are making me cry right now are, _____.

It hurts so much to say this, but when I hear _____, I feel _____.

Take Action. List 3 "I statements" *of your own* that you can try this week. Consider using the Me Statements during times of deep emotional roadblocks in your relationship. What I mean is, times when you really do not want to be vulnerable, but you are committed to deeper conversation and moving past recurring arguments.

Go ahead put this book down for a few days. Look for places *to be real* and *commit to using me statements*. Then come back...

Take Action. How did it feel to use Me Statements? Did any breakthroughs in your conversations with your partner occur? If not, could you see that by perfecting your Me Statements change IS possible? Is using Me Statements way too difficult to imagine, therefore you did not try? What would it take to try making and using Me Statement?

### *STOP: Time to take some notes!*

If you cannot figure out how to create a Me Statement, may I suggest a few sessions with a therapist? Not forever, just two or three sessions. Explain to the therapist that you are attempting to learn how to say and use Me Statements with your partner; they will know what you mean. You will need to be willing to be vulnerable this takes trust. Go easy, start slow. Listening includes learning to listen to yourself.

### Last Little Bit About Listening

If you skipped the rest of the chapter read this list only! To create space for listening with your partner:

1. Sit and face one another.
2. Look into each other's eyes.
3. Hold hands.
4. Continue to make eye contact, even when you feel uncomfortable.
5. Slow down.
6. Allow conversations to unfold in their own time.
7. Don't rush each other.
8. Aim for an uninterrupted hour, best if done once each week.
9. Be open (not defensive).
10. Show empathy.
11. Practice sympathy, yes it IS different from empathy.
12. Learn to paraphrase.
13. Learn to ask for clarification.
14. Do not assume you understand.
15. Try looking, listening, and being present without any words.

> *If it hurts too much to look back, but you're too scared to look ahead, just look beside you and I'll be there.* — Anonymous

Take Action. What listening advice did I miss in the above list that should have been there? Write them down. What advice did I give that you feel is pointless and useless and you are NEVER gonna try it? Write that down.

*STOP: Time to take some notes!*

In sum, in this chapter we studied why listening is more critical than talking, we looked at ideas for not talking throughout a day or more, we tried making active listening an active skill in our repertoire, I introduced deer ears, and ideas around shared listening. We then explored me statements followed up by a few last little hints about listening. In the upcoming chapter my aim is to allow for inclusivity. I had to introduce listening first, so that we can all get into the frame of mind to consider viewpoints different from our own. I believe in all kinds of married and in the next chapter, I plan to tell you what I mean.

# Chapter 3 —
# All Kinds Of Married

> When most people enter marriage, they have only had an "up close and personal" view of a small number of marriages, perhaps only one (i.e., their parents' marriage). Although you likely have known many married people throughout your lifetime, your vision of most marriages is limited to the images that the couples project to the world. You can never really know what another person's marriage is like behind closed doors. Therefore, most people enter into marriage with gaps in their understanding of what marriage entails.
> — Christine E. Murray

## Definitions

There are all kinds of married. My family has a large number of marriages that have been announced to the world in what we, in the West, call traditional ways: vows in the church, the ceremony, the documentation, the party, the honeymoon and so forth.

My aim in this chapter is to explore all kinds of married. I will attempt to reach inclusiveness rather than relying on the existing exclusive meaning of marriage. However, there are many more kinds of marriages and personal commitments than I may be aware of, so please understand I do want to clear the air, somehow, even if with inadequate words.

> One key pattern associated with the development of a close relationship among peers is sustained, escalating, reciprocal, personal self-disclosure. — Arthur Aron and others.

I think we can all agree that committed relationships are a bond between two adult people. The idea of partnerships, marriage, and committed couples is plain and simple right? We seem to agree to an easy statement: "a bond between two adult people."

Sadly, this is not enough. How about heart committed? Admittedly, this is not enough either. I wish that there was an adequate word for all types of adults in bonded and committed relationships, but there is not. Marriage comes close, but it is a word that is strife with political, social, and religious meanings, that do not support all people at this time in history.

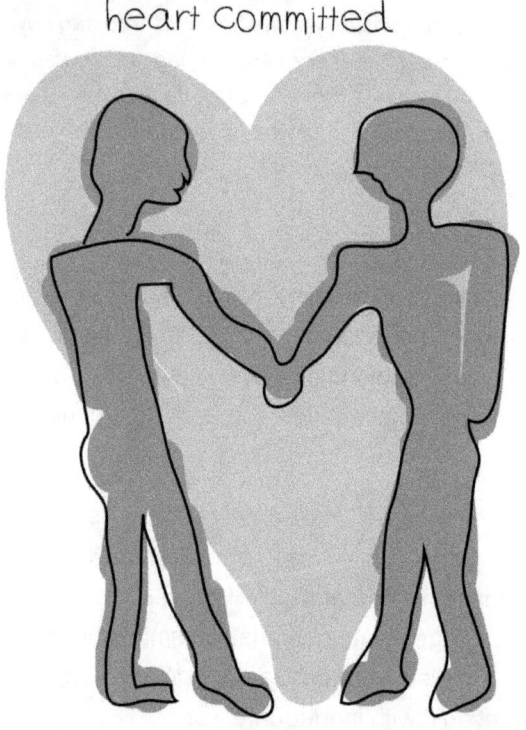

heart committed

I was married by a Priest in a Roman Catholic Church under the umbrella of the Sacrament of Holy Matrimony. This was and is a religious ceremony. The state also required proper documentation for our civil union. Like getting married twice, I suppose. This double entry does not make my commitment to my husband any more valid or true than the millions of committed *relationships that exist in their own form*. A quick historical search and you can find dozens of types of marriages, including types of wedlock I never even considered until I wrote this book.

There are so many different kinds of married, that I could never give a comprehensive list. Marriage can be defined in terms of theology, philosophy, sociology, law, the consent of each party, tradition, and possibly even in other ways I have not thought of here. Allow me to focus on: the consent of each party. *Consent is a living breathing commitment expressed in ongoing growth with one another.* To me, this means agreeing again and again and again and again and again to be with one another: not a one-time ceremony. Not a piece of paper. Not a judge or a court of law. Consent means you agree to be together; each and every day, with each breath.

Allow me to state the definition of the term "consent" again:

> *Consent is a living breathing commitment expressed in ongoing growth with one another.*

Have you consented to be with your partner? Are you committed? Have you expressed the commitment and consent? Are you willing to grow with one another and help each other to grow? Are you a living breathing adult? And is your partner also living and breathing? For lack of a better American word this is marriage.

I believe in **all kinds of married**. My belief, as you can imagine, goes against many of my family members' beliefs. My beliefs also go against the Roman Catholic Church. I have often been silent on this subject at family gatherings and even around my friends. Living my authentic life takes courage. Unfortunately, I am not as courageous as I might like, so, sometimes listening has been my default way of being.

> However, I do support the crazy thought that everyone should have equal rights. Everyone.

Publicly stating that I believe in all kinds of married probably even somehow goes against my marriage vows! There are scriptures, laws, and rules according to the Catholic Church doctrine where I am not supposed to believe in other kinds of married. However, I cannot condone this type of judgment on others. I believe in personal responsibility and taking action for all in the form of kindness and courage. I have the courage to say that there are all kinds of married and all kinds of committed and faithful relationships (today, I have found my courage in writing ☺).

Again, consent is a living breathing commitment expressed in ongoing growth with one another.

When my family members read this book many will be horribly disappointed in my point of view. Even my husband's point of view is different from my own. However, the God I know, the one I pray to, and believe in does not pass judgment on Love, Commitment, and the Consent of partnership between two adults.

> There is an expiry date on blaming your parents for steering you in the wrong direction; the moment you are old enough to take the wheel, responsibility lies with you.
> — J.K. Rowling

So, if you committed to your relationship in a boat, at the top of a rocky cliff, or on a fishing trip — great. If you made a commitment, like I did with a religious celebration, ok then we have something in common. If you committed to your relationship with a verbal contract for a set period of time, to be renewed or broken at the end of the contract — fantastic, good for you. If you are in a partnership that includes being humble and honest with one another and sharing your inner most qualities, bravo well done. If you are a couple that puts your union above your work life, jobs, and other distractions, then bless you for taking care of one another. If you and your partner in life have waited years and years to get a marriage license, I am sorry and I hope our society catches up to the reality of loving relationships of all kinds. To all of you living in beautiful committed partnerships — congratulations.

Married. Husband. Committed Partnership. Wife. Lover. Partnership. Legal union. Significant Other. Domestic Partner. There are all sorts of nuances in all of these words and many other words similar in nature. This book gladly embraces all kinds of committed relationships, regardless of word choice. I do not want to leave anyone out, please accept my deepest apologies if I inadvertently say something offensive to some group due to my poor word choices. I plan to keep learning and growing and I am human. If I could invent a new word that encompasses the love I feel for courageous men and women who consent to committing to a life-long bond with one another, I would. We are currently wallowing in controversy that need not be so.

If you're committed, you know it. I am glad you are here and I welcome comments, suggestions, and feedback so that I can learn more and share more. My knowledge is a work in progress and I am happy to have conversations about communication and relationship building. My need to share this information is strong, but I know there will be gaps in my understanding of other couples' foibles, problems, successes, and joys.

> *And that's how it is for most of us now with our belief systems: they're different from each other, and relatively complicated.*
> *— John C. Parkin*

I know there are gaps in my understanding of consent and marriage too! But it is not my job to pass judgment on other peoples commitments to one another and I hope that one day we can embrace all kinds of married.

If this book could heal, help, inspire, or otherwise entertain any couples across the globe to participate in conversations and laughter I would be delighted. If by building stronger relationships through communication we collectively build a more beautiful, gentle, and kind society I would feel that some of my life's work is taking hold.

During my research for this book I came across a researcher who used children's ideas of marriage to gain some insight. This researcher asked many kids to give their ideas on marriage; I love Kenny's response:

> It gives me a headache to think about that stuff. I'm just a kid. I don't need that kind of trouble. — Kenny, age 7

What if we stay out of each other's business? What if laws could change that supported consenting committed adults; allowing them to stay together for life, supporting one another and growing in love?

Allow me to add one more thought to this topic. In honor of Kenny and all the other children in the world, if your commitment includes bringing children into the circle of consent, please stay true to one another and give the children a loving safe home. Children are little people without a voice in divorce, and this pains me. They need to feel secure and loved unconditionally by both people who are their parents. Your commitment should include staying together once the children have been brought into the circle of trust and consent.

Take Action. Remember I told you I would be presenting many questions, well here we go! The conversation starter for this chapter is: Discuss with one another what all of these words mean to you and list couples you know that fit or do not fit into conventional categorization. What are some of the categorizing words I missed? Can you think of a better and brand new word for marriage that is inclusive to all types of committed and consenting adults?

*STOP: Time to take some notes!*

Heart Committed, Married, Husband, Committed Partnership, Wife, Lover, Partnership, Spouse, Domestic Partner, Legal union, Significant Other, and Other _____.

Take Action. Further questions. Define if and how any of these categorizations fit your own expectations for your relationship to each other. Whew, a biggie!

Use love and compassion while exploring these terms for relationships. Remember, we are looking for a more beautiful, gentle, and kind society. Search for meaning through love and compassion. The change starts with you. What change do you want to see? What have I said here that to you feels wrong? Why?

*STOP: Time to take some notes!*

Heart Committed, Married, Husband, Committed Partnership, Wife, Lover, Partnership, Spouse, Domestic Partner, Legal union, Significant Other, and Other _____.

What is your definition of "married"? Do you feel like it was necessary to single out the topic of marriage as a chapter in a book about conscious curiosity and asking each other questions to increase communication, collaboration and cash flow? If so, why? If not, why not?

In the next chapter we are going to unlock the truth about serious committed relationships and then we'll grow our knowledge of what makes a powerful partnership. When boundaries are set and the bond between you grows, you will be ready for a relationship playdate and taking on leadership in your life together. But first, let's explore truth, truth in committed relationships.

## Chapter 4 —
## Truth: Bring Out the Best

*A flower cannot blossom without sunshine and man cannot live without love.* — Max Muller

I am going to be honest and up front, as I will keep doing throughout this book. I am worried about this chapter. I am worried about using a loaded word such as "Truth," because titling a chapter "Truth" can invariably get me into a situation where one day, one of my statements will actually be *false*. Truth can be multi-dimensional, but we tend to think of it in terms of one dimension—things are either true or they are not true.

Worried.

With this in mind, please know that I dug deep into what I know to be true for me today and now. I wrote these down, tested them by reading them out loud to myself regularly and discussing the statements with my husband and others. The statements I tested became My Truth List. My truth list is what I know and believe to be true about committed relationships, today and at the time of publishing this book.

## Truth List

I am eager for others to share their truths and to have conversations with me, with others, and with their significant other about whether My Truth List is indeed really true. Having said that, I am ready to share my list of Truths about relationships:

1. You cannot just "want" a relationship; you need to be open to the enormous change any relationship brings to your life. Taking responsibility as an adult means that sometimes the change needs to come from within you. Read between the lines: No partner will walk into your life asking you to mold him or her into your vision of a perfect partner!
2. You cannot live 100% in your own style, brain, way, and actions — collaboration, give and take, and occasional compromise are all integral parts of commitment. You either give and take or break!
3. Conversely, you cannot live as 1% or only 99% of yourself. Collaboration and compromise, when done with attention to your heart and brain, help you to grow to BE 100% yourself. Your partner deserves all of you to be true.
4. A great partner can help make you better than you ever thought possible. Yes, you can expect a great partner to see you as and encourage you to be a better You.
5. "My way or the highway" — never works.
6. You need to choose to commit to the relationship every day that you wake up, every hour, every minute, and maybe even every nano-second. What I am saying here is that "to commit," does not mean you are done. You

may have pledged your life to someone, but that pledge needs to be constantly renewed. To commit is to do, to carry out, and to decide over and over again that you want keep what you put into action.
7. Marriage is not a wedding.
8. A committed relationship can make you a stronger individual. A timid, weak or broken spirited individual rarely, if ever, makes a relationship stronger.
9. Know and keep learning what you need to sustain YOU. Make sure to take care of YOU in order to support the WE.
10. Boys and girls really do converse differently, but gender does not really matter — all individuals have their own special way of communicating. The magic is in finding the connection.
11. Trust is a funny word. Once trust is broken, both parties must expend a herculean amount of energy if trust is ever to be re-built. Better not to break trust in the first place, not ever.
12. Let him or her Go For It! Sometimes, one person in the relationship needs to step aside to let the other person grow for a week, a month, a year or two, occasionally more. I don't mean go away and commit stupid acts against the commitment of the relationship. What I am talking about here is personal growth. Things like further education, time alone, and personal adventures. Then the couple, most especially the one who stayed behind needs to allow for "re-entry" into the relationship. This process can take up to six months or more, depending on the circumstances. It's important to know that healthy relationships may need these times of slightly altered focus on one of the two people. This is not about growing away from one another. The growth that can

happen is about the individuals within the couple. Ultimately the couple grows and bonds more strongly. To allow a partner to Go For It, both people will need to give it time, patience, and love. Don't forget to check in frequently.
13. There is much good in allowing and encouraging each other to keep learning and following personal interests. Together is great, but at the end of the day, being able to share some alternative view of the world helps both parties to grow, learn, and be fuller human beings.
14. We all have different speeds in life. Remember the story of the Tortoise and the Hare? The tortoise is slow and the hare is fast? People too, have different speeds. Not only that, our own personal speed could change during our life or for certain activities in life. In a committed relationship, having trust in each other's speed of going forward in life is critical. The truth is, blocking or speeding up your partner for your own motives is a terrible waste of time and energy. The deeper truth is, this is harder to spot than you can ever imagine, therefore be mindful of the Tortoise and the Hare.

## Looking for Truth

I encourage you to grow your own truth list. To aid you in this process I want you to think of your relationship in terms of a garden. This exercise is titled: Looking for Truth in A Soulful Relationship Garden. A well-tended garden, especially a pesticide-free garden, creates a healthy ecosystem in which plants, bugs, worms, and more thrive and grow in abundance.

Conscious Curiosity | 89

Relationship Garden

I encourage you to imagine of all the wonderful creatures, plants, bugs, and mosses that grow in a thriving garden. For example: honey bees, bugs, beetles, nits, dirt, soil, weeds, flowers, water, sun, worms, vegetables, fruits, trees, vines, fertilizer, birds, lizards, bunnies and other critters. Take the time to consider each of these beautiful helpful elements of a thriving eco-system and relate them to your own relationship. Be literal and be creative.

Take Action. Are the roots of the trees your ancestors? What have they taught you about the truth of relationships? Is the dirt your history or your future? How does the sun and water hinder or nurture your relationship garden? What do the huge sunflowers reaching to the sky say about your growth as a couple? What do the buzzing bees and hummingbirds that go around sucking nectar and leaving pollen say about give and take in your relationship? What about those zillions of aphids, what do they represent? Are the weeds truth bombs? Is there stuff you know needs to be addressed, like the weeds in a garden, but golly gosh, the work sucks! Dig, tend, and grow your truth. ...and no fair using pesticides!

*STOP: Time to take some notes!*

Let's continue on the garden path here for a while.

## Time, Resources, Boundaries

Gardens have times of growth and rebirth. Gardens tend to reach new edges and push boundaries when they are healthy or even retreat when they are suffering from lack of care. Mosses creep slowly and grow slowly seeking the nutrients they need to survive and prosper. Weeds grow wherever they please, even up though cracks in cement or on top of scattered debris.

Take Action. What can gardens teach you about cycles in your relationship? What can you learn from the boundaries or the edges of the garden? Remember, you are looking for truth. What is true for you in your relationship?

*STOP: Time to take some notes!*

Let's take a moment to look at another factor of communication that affects your relationship over time. Direct or indirect communication can either grow or reduce resources, and may create unwanted boundaries between you and your partner. Direct communication is often perceived as authoritative.

In a garden, an example of direct use of resources and boundaries is when a great leafy tree over a grassy area kills the grass. Without the direct sun needed under the tree, the grass is stunted. Many plants cannot grow in shade, but some thrive in this environment. The tree knows what it needs and gets it. The plants under the tree that survive are well suited to their environment.

Indirect communication in a garden, in my mind, is similar to the symbiotic relationship found in healthy ecosystems. A fallen dead tree gives life to abundant plants, microorganisms, bugs, and even animals. But even with the indirect giving or communication with the rest of the garden, the tree is still dead. The tree can take and give in the same garden at different times in its life cycle. When it was alive it was in direct communication with the ecosystem. What the tree does is grow and change in all it's life cycles. Trees do stuff that might go unseen and yet all of this is a healthy part of garden activity and growth. Indirect communication is commonly thought of as more polite. Direct communication is often thought of as more forceful. In a garden, neither direct nor indirect contributions are more important — life is important. I believe there is a time and place for both direct and indirect communication.

In your relationship be aware of both indirect and direct communication and when one or the other is more appropriate to the life of your relationship.

Direct Communication examples:
I am telling you...
I hear what you are saying but I am asking you to...

Indirect Communication examples:
Can you reach...
Do you know of...
Can you remind me of...
Could you...

Take Action. Consider when and if direct communication is the best way to talk to your partner. In what scenarios would it be most appropriate? Can indirect communication be misleading or confusing? For me, sometimes when I genuinely use a question such as: Do you know of any new good movies? My husband will immediately assume I want to go to the movies! When in reality I may have been simply asking a question to open conversation.

I opened this section with a focus on time, resources, and boundaries. Is it fair to ask an indirect question when you know that the question will lead to a longer argument? Should you knowingly direct your partner to do something that uses their resources that does not support them, only supports yourself? Can being indirect lead to issues of ill-defined boundaries? My husband is accustomed to responding to indirect communication with rapid-fire action! I need to be careful of what I say or he may jump up and act, even when I do not need him to! This tendency comes from how he was raised. What can you notice about the different uses of direct and indirect communication in your relationship?

*STOP: Time to take some notes!*

Once you have given the topic of time, resources, and boundaries a fair shake, then it is time to plan some fun!

## Relationship Playdate

I cannot think of a better place to have a relationship playdate than in a garden. Can you? Well, ok a bedroom might be another place to have some play, yes! Ok, but this book is about conscious curiosity and communicating to connect. We are in the truth chapter so, let's look for truth using conscious curiosity in seriously fun places.

> *You can discover more about a person in an hour of play than in a year of conversation.* — Plato

Take Action. In this chapter, focus and look for personal and relationship truth bombs. Truth bombs are those things you try to ignore, but you know they are there and you know that the ideas, preconceived or ill-conceived, affect your relationship every single day. Look for truth bombs. What is TRUE for you and for both of you as a team? What is so true that is hurts? Those are the things to lovingly open up to. Nurture. Discuss. Cry about together. Find healing, by being open, honest, and kind to one another.

I am going to ask you to schedule a Relationship Playdate. Go ahead and put this book down as soon as you finish this paragraph. Go mark your calendar in ink with your significant other, pick a day, then beginning planning for fun.

Did you put a date on your calendars? Yes, ok. Keep the date and keep on reading.

On your playdate make sure you go outside! Frolic in a garden. Lie down on grass and look at clouds together. Sit under a tree and feel the strength of the trunk jabbing you in your back as the worthy bark of a great oak or flowing willow remind you of stability and patience. Take in ocean breezes together. Visit a nursery that is beyond the boundaries of your town. Go to a park. Visit a playground meant for kids, but go at a time were you are assured some time on the play structures for a few fun minutes without the children present. Visit a working farm and pet some animals, watch them, what do they have to teach you? You could visit a zoo and discuss how the boundaries of zoo animal cages changes the life of the animals. Visit a botanical garden in your area, including off-season visits. What does nature have to offer?

Play outside.

Think of your own special place to visit and search for truth that rings true for both of you. Search also for those awful truth bombs that are inhibiting your relationship from being the best and most fulfilling partnership.

> The best way to find happiness as a couple is to first attain it as individuals. — Dora Ficher

Take Action. Write, draw, or take pictures during your playdate. Take a GoPro camera and be silly together. Record the wonder of being together in fun. Discover truth according to you. The truth is, I hope you have fun.

**STOP: Time to take some notes and pictures!**

If you are like me, you may also bring a sketchbook and create deeper memories through drawing and writing about your playdate. I sincerely hope you take me up on this idea and play like a child, enjoy each other's company. Most of all, enjoy searching for truth. Next up, leadership.

## Leadership

So often we think about leadership as something to be used in a business stetting. As a way to gain a higher income or more prestige in our job, as way to gain notoriety in volunteer organizations, and even as a way to win awards in the pursuit of hobbies. What if you decided to lead yourself into being a person that you could wake up each day feeling proud of — not just at work — but also at home and with the people you love the most. What would that type of leadership look like? What would you have to do to be a leader in and of your life?

What is leadership? How do you define leadership? How would you begin to harness your leadership skills to strengthen your primary relationship and the relationships to the people you love.

**STOP: Time to take some notes!**

Create a definition of leadership. List 5 words that best describe the type of leader you want to be for yourself, and with your partner and family.

For me, focusing on my own happiness, well-being, and emotional intelligence is the first step in creating a great relationship with my husband, children, and extended family. I am a leader through being my own leader, by taking responsibility for the life I have created through the choices I make. I seriously hope you take the idea of leadership and apply it to your life at home as seriously as you might have honed your leadership skills for work.

> *In the long run, we shape our lives, and we shape ourselves. The process never ends until we die. And the choices we make are ultimately our own responsibility.*
> 
> — Eleanor Roosevelt

My aim in this chapter was to help you to bring out the best of you through exploring what you think is true about relationships. In sum, what did you think about the truth list and looking for truth? If any of the ideas seemed really off or wrong to you, journal about this and take the time to explore your ideas and feelings. Remember, this book is written for you to tap into your curiosity and improve your relationship with your significant other. What did you learn in this chapter that made you feel off kilter, why?

I also introduced the ideas of time, resources, and boundaries and what this means in a committed relationship. If you have any further personal thoughts, jot them down. The idea behind asking you to take a relationship playdate is literally to have fun, like a child would or to play together in a way you likely used to early on in your relationship. Once you know how great it feels to play with your partner, take leadership and responsibility for the fun in your life and grow some more homespun fun.

Next up we have... you guessed it! More questions! I am so sure that the playdate opened up wells of desire to learn and grow and know more about each other so I devised a conversation starters chapter — I titled the chapter: Trophy relationship or Real Relationship. Read on to find out why. The content is ready and waiting for you on the next page.

# Chapter 5 —
# Trophy Relationship or Real Relationship

*Love is a partnership of two unique people who bring out the very best in each other, and who know that even though they are wonderful as individuals, they are even better together.*
— Barbara Cage

## Saying It Is Not Living It

This Conversation Starters chapter is the continuation of a booklet I wrote and published (for one couple) over 20 years ago! Only now, over 20 years into my own marriage am I ready to expand my initial thoughts. Marriage looked like it should 20 years ago to me and now I see things from a new and more complex experience base.

I clearly and fully remember my first months of marriage. I enjoyed saying, "This is my husband, Derek." I remember the thrill and excitement that came along with using those words. I felt like I had captured a grownup rite of passage or an adult trophy.

Soon, reality reared its ugly head. Peacocking the words, "my husband" was not the same as making things work behind closed doors at home for the two of us. Somewhere between the thrill and the reality came the knowledge that the real relationship was going to take a lot of effort and many joint memories and much more than saying; "This is my husband."

> *On Marriage: ...there probably aren't many people whose idea of 24-hour-a-day good times consists of being yoked to the same romantic partner, through bouts of stomach flu and depression, financial setbacks and emotional upsets, until after many a long decade, one or the other eventually dies in harness.* — Caitlin Flanagan

During this time, it occurred to me that the first moments and months of my relationship with my husband would be lost if I did not actively attempt to remember stuff. I began writing questions, making illustrations and I shared my ideas about capturing strange memories, in a small book format, with a newlywed couple — as a gift. They never did tell me what they thought of the book. Then again, I never asked!

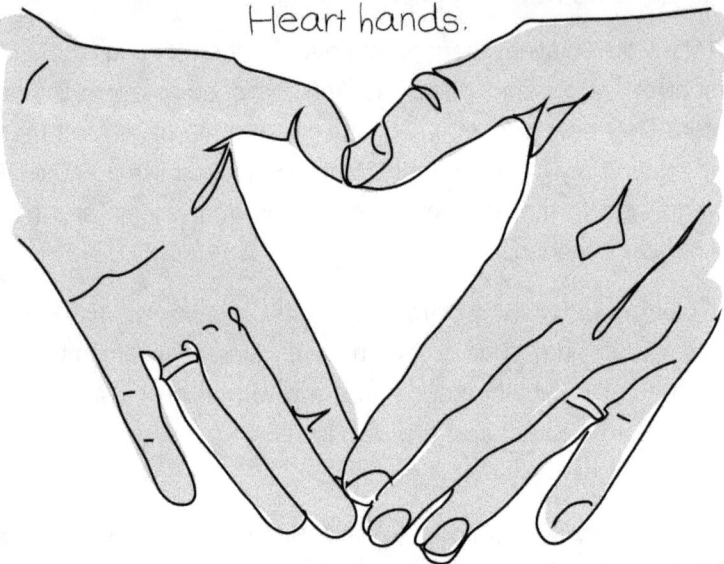

Heart hands.

Over the years I lost track of this little book that I had created (I knew I had kept myself a copy, but I did not know where I had stashed it). The words and images I had made kept tickling my inner muse, where was that project and how could I find it? Finally, I absolutely had to pay attention to the tickle. I was eager to find deeper connection with my husband, so why not start from the beginning? I decided to do a major deep cleaning of my studio in order to find my copy of the book that I had given to a newlywed couple so long ago.

*Remember that great love and great achievements involve great risk.*

Originally, the book was presented as rudimentary drawings and conversation starters, all done by hand, with no technology involved. It was less than 16 pages long. It was done on ordinary white drawing paper. Deep cleaning and searching did the trick! I did find my copy of conversation starters! Now, I can share it here, with additional questions, statements, pages and ideas that I have written and illustrated more recently. You know what? I have even dredged up some fond memories of my first days with my love.

I hope you find that you have lots to say and learn about one another. I am asking you to record your thoughts, comments, ideas, and laughter as you go through the pages. I wish I had recorded more of what happened in our first days and months together. But I did not. However, I have found that, you can rekindle the memories through following the questions outlined in this chapter and throughout this book.

Keep asking questions. Questions keep the conversation going.

Curiosity shows interest.

Take Action. Find a comfortable place to hang out with each other for about an hour or so. Be open to one person being the scribe, and the other person talking. Switch roles. Record your juicy conversational pleasures. You will find that sometimes ideas are easier to share if each of you allow time for written reflection instead of talking first. Yes, go ahead and read the silliness and seriousness of the questions posed in this chapter of Conscious Curiosity. Use your words and your newly practiced listening skills. Then record these precious thoughts with your images and words.

The Conversation Starters chapter is about filling your love box full of memories. Like the quotation at the beginning of this chapter, your box is empty until you fill the void with you and we, together, and love. So let's begin, ask yourselves, what kind of couple do you want to be?

## What Kind of Couple Do We Want to Be?

How do we want others to characterize us? Consider words such as: honest, kind, generous, responsible, sensitive, silly, considerate, loyal, accountable, fun, lively, active, fascinating, frustrating, closed, open, smart, and so on…come up with three special words to describe each individual. Then find three words to describe the kind of couple you want to be to the world and why.

Take Action. Whittle your thoughts down to two, or three words that best describe the way you want to present yourself and yourselves as a couple to the world.

> *STOP: Time to take some notes!*

I present myself as: _____

We present ourselves as: _____

What happens to your characterizations of yourself and of your relationship if you present yourselves only to each other, not the whole world? Did/do the words and ideas change? Why?

> honest, kind, generous, responsible, humorous, considerate, loyal, accountable, fun, lively, active, fascinating, frustrating, closed, giving, empathetic, open, smart, other...

Does how you present yourself as an individual align with how you present yourselves as a couple? Why or why not?

Why is it important to think about what kind of couple you want to be? Or is this exercise entirely useless?

You may find that you want to come back to these questions once you've completed the next section: Conversation Starter Questions. Hopefully, you will learn that there is still so very much to learn about each other. Good Luck!

## Conversation Starter Questions

What are some of the first things you can remember about me when we met for the first time?

What areas in our relationship are thriving?

What are our strengths?

What are our opportunities?

What do we do really well together?

What would you say is the *most* romantic thing I have ever done for you? Have you shared a chocolate bar on a fishing trip?

Where do we excel?

What is crucial in our relationship?

What are some challenges?

What seems to come up over and over again?

What does "being partners" mean?

If you knew you could not have sex for the next 6 years, what would you do to make the marriage work (hint: see image above)?

Zen Habits — things that will not change unless they change. What do you need within the relationship to feel whole, alive, and worthy of being loved?

What part of my body do you enjoy most?

Labels — what do they really mean? Trophy husband/wife, stay at home mom/dad, husband/wife, partner/spouse/significant other, step -son, -daughter, -mother, -father, -aunt, -uncle, lesbian, gay, bisexual? Seriously, there are so many labels out there. Learn about each other's definitions of these words. When you do not know each other's definition, problems may ensue. Take the time to learn what the labels mean to each of you. Seek clarification. Have a conversation.

In what way do you want to change the world? What have you done in the past year to make the change happen? Month? Week? Today? How much time, money and energy are you willing to spend to change the world?

How's my kissing?

hot · icy · aged · bitter
salty · sweet · sloppy · smooth
sophisticated · wet · dry · childish

How would you describe our first kiss?

Name three bottom line relationship killers. Name three top items that could greatly enhance the relationship in this moment.

What is old and heavy and needs to be heaved, hoed, and released? Write the thing(s) here. On another date together write the old and heavy items needing to be released on a rock(s). Go to a lake, pond, river, ocean or other body of water and do a rock-tossing contest. I warn you, this can be very fun!

Name three things I have done today that you love?

Suppose that a movie were going to be made about you. Imagine the Hollywood lights! Who do you think would be most suited to play you in the movie? Why? What kind of movie, play, concert, or musical would you like to star in? Give details.

Why did this book catch your attention? Maybe the book did not catch your attention; maybe it infuriates you, why?

What is the silliest or off-the-wall stunt you have ever done in your life?

Parachute Jumping

What stunt do you dream of doing that I should know about beforehand?

If you were not answering these endless questions right now what would you rather be doing?

Maybe you want more questions? Arthur Aron of the Interpersonal Relationships Lab at Stony Brook University in New York, stipulates that increased intimacy, even with those whom you already know, can be fostered through a set of 36 questions that he and others with him devised. Aron is a social psychology researcher (with others), who published a paper titled, "The Experimental Generation of Interpersonal Closeness" in Personality and Social Psychology. They believe they have devised the 36 questions that can bring you closer together. So, in case you feel that I have not provided enough questions, please check out his work (the questions can be found online).

What was the first thing that came to your mind when you saw me naked for the first time?

You are an adult now and adults tend to hide from stuff they least like about themselves. What do you regularly try to hide? What do you think is fair game to hide from one another? What if you did not hide from what is it that you choose to hide, how would life be richer? Poorer?

Fears — sometimes you do not even recognize them, but they are there! Look for patterns. Write some down. What are your biggest fears in relation to your relationship? We are not talking about spiders or public speaking, but of deeper inner fears that you imagine you cannot tell a soul. To share these fears is incredibly risky and when listened to with compassion can be incredibly beautiful. What are you most afraid of?

Lost your toys?

Imagine you lost ALL your toys and your job — including our house — how would you begin to re-measure your definition of success? Please note, I realize that this question hits close to home for many couples that lived through the recent 2008 recession. However, having a conversation about this topic allows couples a chance to reflect on what went well, how recovery happened at a private level, and to gain strength from the adversity that we all experienced.

> *This is all you have. This is not a dry run. This is your life. If you want to fritter it away with your fears, then you will fritter it away, but you won't get it back later.* — Dr. Laura Schlessinger

Enough! Enough already! Did you get the idea around being consciously curious here? Did I present plenty of conversation starter questions? Do you have any of your own I should have asked?

Let's move on. Relationships are often thought of as liner. I'd like to think we are more than a continuum of linear decisions. The following section introduces the idea of relationship intersections. These are times when yield signs, stop signs and green lights abound.

## Relationship Intersections

Life lessons and the chaos often found during relationship intersections can be more easily handled when you spend time alone in introspection. What I mean is, each of us has a timeline of life events. Like a city road we move along until we hit a traffic signal. The signal forces us to stop whether we want to or not. In life, the stop signs and traffic signals are many and varied. Examples are: sickness, death, loss of income, marriage, new jobs, return to education, family crisis, moving, and many other so called "stressful times."

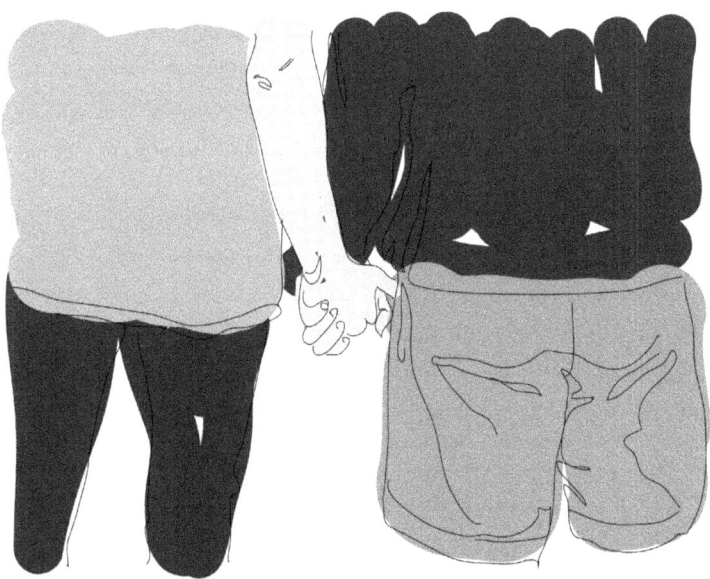

There will always be occasions when unusual and/or customary life intersections punctuate one's relationship. While the intersections are happening sometimes the feelings can be enjoyed and other times can be seriously challenging, and upsetting. The latter is usually more common. However, when viewed in retrospect, I suspect that the "good times" in your relationship have usually happened at intersections of life events. While the challenges may feel insurmountable at the time that they are being presented to you in life, in retrospect I am quite sure you will see intersections as "The Good Times" and the "Times to Remember." Why? Because it is through adversity that we grow, change, learn, and feel better about ourselves. Rough spots help us to grow our self-esteem. Even sickness and death creates room for more knowing about the joys of life.

The point of this conversation starter section about intersections is to begin to recognize those beautiful, crazy, complicated, and congested times in life — often called "life's ups and downs." In any given year there is bad stuff and good stuff, the same is true each month, each week, each day and even every hour. What will you do to notice the beauty of intersections? Will you take out your phone at a red light and text someone or will you look ahead on the road at all the opportunities?

Take Action. Can you think of any intersections in your relationship? Meaning…times when one person was on a path to something and the other person was on a path towards something else, and you thought, this is it, this is when the world we know will all come crumbling down. And yet, "It All Worked Out!"

Are there times that you can remember that you thought everything was going wrong, but in retrospect things turned out for the best? Are there any intersections where both people in the relationship were suffering their own personal hell, but when looked at with some distance, the wisdom that came from that intersection helped you grow deeper together? Write some ideas about intersections in life down, and celebrate these moments.

> *STOP: Time to take some notes! Celebrate the intersections.*

Are there any times in your life together that the intersection was jam-packed with all of the good stuff of life? Can you name times when both of you felt alive, loved, and supported? You remember thinking to yourself, "Wow, this is all too good to be true." When will something go wrong? How can we keep juggling all this good stuff? Take the time to relish these memories. Look at pictures or draw images of the things that happened during these times. Is there any way to recapture some of the joy of a full and beautiful intersection?

What is real, the horrible times or the joyful times? If you were to give each other a trophy, what event or events would deserve a trophy? Why?

Intersections are designed to improve the flow of traffic. Keep this in mind next time you feel an intersection in your life with your partner. Stop, look, and proceed with caution. However, stop dead highway traffic is a whole other problem and is usually caused by collisions preceded by careless driving.

If you feel like you are on a collision path with your partner, please do yourself and your relationship a favor and seek expert help, the information in this book will not be enough to stop the oncoming wreckage and potential death of the relationship.

Real people being really honest create great relationships. You deserve a great relationship, go out and make it happen. Don't feed the idea of a trophy relationship; look for the potential of a real relationship. How? Let's move on to care and feeding of relationships.

## Care and Feeding

No, this is not Dr. Laura's version of care and feeding! (Dr. Laura Schlessinger wrote the famous book: The Proper Care and Feeding of Husbands.) We are working on the care and feeding of your relationship. Specifically in relation to thinking about what constitutes a real relationship versus a trophy relationship. And, as I promised you at the beginning of this book, I have many more questions than answers. Are you finding answers yet? I sure hope so! Taking care of your partner and feeding your relationship is not only the job of a wife! Seriously, let's create a new model! What does care and feeding of a relationship really mean?

Take Action. How do you feed your relationship? Do you talk for a minimum of one hour per week? Do you argue with assertive sensitivity? Do you forgive and apologize with sincerity? Do you change your behavior as necessary? Do you praise changed behavior in your partner? Do you go on dates? Do you work as hard on your relationship as you do on your work, career, fitness, and other life activities? Do you pray together? Do you dream together? List at least 5 things you can try in the next few months that will feed your relationship. Take care of the "we" and your relationship can thrive!

*STOP: Time to take some notes!*

Define romance. What does romance mean for you and your partner? What feels romantic? How can you *be* romantic when you find that your definition of romance differs from your partners' views? In your notes come up with and list 5 or more romantic activities. As a bonus, take out your calendars and together schedule and commit to a few romantic activities in ink for the next six months to a year. Make some of the events short and sweet. Make other events day long, week-long, or even create and dream a bigger romance activity or trip.

> *Frankly, too many women treat their husbands as accessories instead of priorities. — Dr. Laura Schlessinger*

Did you ever want to travel to all 7 continents together? Did you ever consider a trip around the world on a motorcycle? That's what my husband wants to do. Will we? Not sure, but as I write this I wonder why I was so hesitant when he told me this dream! The truth sometimes hurts (see the Dr. Laura quote above).

The truth is, is he still a trophy to me, or can I help him reach his dream and make this a *real* relationship? Can we somehow travel on a motorcycle far enough to satisfy him and his dream? Can we travel around the world without a motorcycle? Can we dig deeper and find out what it is about a motorcycle trip that he thinks would be so satisfying? I am not sure, but it is probably worth a try.

### *STOP: Time to take some notes!*

What are you living in, a trophy relationship or a real relationship? Which would you rather have? How can you move towards what you really want?

In sum, Saying It Is Not Living It — if you want a truly fulfilling relationship you need to live it, every day and every moment and even behind closed doors. Start by choosing: What Kind of Couple Do You Want to Be? Then, as we discussed, have conversations, often. Never be afraid to spend time alone in order to be better together. And remember that the care and feeding of your relationship is worth your time if you really want to be in a real relationship.

We have been through a ton of information in this book so far. To recap, you now know:

1. The sage advice of my mother: communication, collaboration, cash and faith
2. Stuff about the hard work, creating dreams, looking inside, and coming out
3. The power of talking and listening
4. A whole heck of a lot about listening
5. There are different kinds of marriage
6. Truth brings out the best in a relationship
7. Conversations build trust, intimacy, and shared histories

Incidentally, love is built and thrives through trust and intimacy.

The next chapter is the big kahuna: I call it Mastermind Planning. I have divided life into 20 categories for you to explore as a couple. The next chapter is *big* work. The next chapter is where you can create waves of change in your relationship. If you have been honestly working to better understand each other up to this point, mastermind planning will probably be fun. Maybe some people will jump to the chapters that interest them the most and start with mastermind planning, that's fine by me, but I think the content will be easier to tackle if the foundation was set using the work from the previous chapters. Good luck, I hope you enjoy the process of unlocking your best life together in the next chapter: Mastermind Planning.

# Chapter 6 —
# Mastermind Planning

> *You have brains in your head. You have feet in your shoes. You can steer yourself in any direction you choose. You're on your own, and you know what you know. And you are the guy who'll decide where to go.* — Dr. Seuss

## The Treasure Hunt

This chapter, in my mind, is the BIG work. I see so many places in our world and on-line that people take individual self-help courses and business improvement classes to create a better life for — one person — themselves. What I have failed to find is Mastermind Planning for Couples. Mastermind planning can be like an enormous treasure hunt designed for you and your partner. The treasure hunt is the joy in uncovering precious dreams and goals and making plans to set your life in motion together — in other words, Mastermind Planning for Couples.

As far as I know, using the idea of mastermind planning for couples is not a commonplace practice. I have looked around for clues that this is happening. With a quick check on-line you can access mastermind success principles and guidelines for businesses or individuals in business, but not for couples. I have decided to use the term Mastermind Planning because it has occurred to me, why can't couples think of themselves as a *unit that could move forward together in unison with determined plans?* This is the dictionary definition of mastermind planning. Shoot, even bank robbers make mastermind plans!

Mastermind groups for organizations and entrepreneurs are organized both in-person and on-line all over the world. Mastermind groups can yield excellent results for those people who are committed to being involved in them and putting forth sustained effort.

In addition to mastermind groups I have also thought a great deal about how every year many people individually set out to create New Year's Resolutions and take the time to do "A year in review lists and/or journal entries." This got me thinking, why can't couples do mastermind planning and/or create determined resolutions together? And since we can and should, why don't we?

This chapter is formatted in such a way that with focused 15 minute to one-hour increments of time, couples can jointly share conversations around important life topics. I would not expect couples to be able to "power through" this chapter in one sitting, there is simply too much to plan and talk about in one afternoon together. I know because I have tried many of the sections of this chapter with my husband. Usually the work took longer than we anticipated.

Bank robbers and business owners take months (sometimes years) to complete powerful mastermind plans. You should expect that creating well-defined plans for your relationship would take work done together and work done on reconnaissance missions, where you gather outside information over time. Mastermind planning is a way of directing a complex project to successful completion. Aren't long-term committed relationships and all ensuing parts and parties in need of expert masterminding? I think so!

> *A mastermind alliance is built of two or more minds working actively together in perfect harmony toward a common definite object.* — Napoleon Hill

This chapter also follows a similar doctrine to organized programs developed by none other than the Catholic Church! My husband and I wanted to marry in the Catholic tradition. Along with that came certain expectations. One such expectation was to attend Engaged Encounter (a Catholic pre-marriage retreat program). In Engaged Encounter the planning strategies are done according to Catholic teachings. Engaged Encounter is an organized program and a way of asking each other hundreds of questions based on the teachings of the church and sharing answers with one another. The program was presented to us in a convent over the course of a long weekend. Many couples did not and do not survive the program. By *not* surviving, I mean that they drop out or give up. Whether they try again or not, I do not know. The intention of the church is to ensure compatibility within the teachings of the church and to ensure that couples go into marriage with full knowledge of the scope of the commitment.

We enjoyed the process. Although, I will admit to experiencing Engaged Encounter as being a thoroughly exhausting adventure! I also feel that no matter how hard the church works to try to prepare a couple for a life-time commitment, there really is no way of knowing all the shit that will fly into the relationship over time. There is also no way of knowing how many wonderful adventures there will be either.

In our first few years of marriage, we found that continuing to talk and plan based on what we had discussed in the Engaged Encounter program was not too hard to follow-up on. We kept writing down our expectations for our life together. We even tried Marriage Encounter (similar to engaged encounter, but designed for married couples) through our church several years later, but we did not last through the weekend. We left. What we found was, we had already devised ways to talk and plan with one another that worked for us without the doctrine of the church.

We have also found that, we usually talk more when we travel, and when camping, picnicking, or hiking. I know I think more clearly when I am outside. My husband enjoys hardy physical activity interspersed with talking. We continue to talk about how we wanted to build our future together. The world in front of us continues to feel like an open-slate for dreams to be written. Long ago, we were young and very much in love, and through a homespun version of mastermind planning we continued to feel the wonder of future opportunities.

About 5 years after our marriage, we had children.

Finding time for future planning, while we raised our kids, was hectic and crazy. Often we lived day-to-day and fell into exhausted sleep whenever possible. When we remembered to, we would look back at our earlier dreamy notes of what we planned for our family. This activity was rare. Sometimes, we surprised ourselves and realized we had accomplished some of our dreams. Other times we realized that, no, a particular dream may never happen — too lofty, too expensive, not right for the way the family was evolving or whatever else. The best were times when we could implement yet another task or adventure that we had dreamed of 5 or 10 years previously. Life has brought us to yet another juncture. Now we are actively working on even more new and wonderful adventures to enjoy with one another.

## Change Is Inevitable

Life is change. This book, in part, started because my husband and I are at yet another life transition and change. Both of our children will be leaving for college soon. There are all sorts of emotions around the idea of having been a family of 4 for almost two decades back down to a family of 2 for much of the year. Our children are beginning to find their own way in the world. That gives us space and time to rediscover each other and find our own new way in the world.

This process of negotiating life changes is on-going and never finished.

You cannot plan for change, but you can change your plans. The work in this chapter will take hours and hours of reading, thinking, writing, and talking. The work in this chapter may even take some outside research using expert opinions, friends, family, and the internet. I do not have a magic wand that will grant you the time you will need to follow through on the ideas presented here. What I can promise you is that if you do the work, the results will astonish you. Skipping the possibility and potential that comes from mastermind work is foolish.

Take Action. Think of each of the life area in the following list. At first, simply read the entire list. Then go back and think of what calls to you the most at this time. What needs to be looked at? What is bothersome? What have you failed to look at until you saw this list? Pick any one topic and jump in and give it a try. Or start from the beginning and go through all the topics.

One way that you can approach this planning is to look at actions that can be taken in the next week or month and write them down. Then do them. Another method is to think of the topics in terms of 3 months from now, 1 year, 2 years, 5, 10, 15, and more. Write down any thoughts, goals, ideas, dislikes, and memories from other couples and family members you know. Use this information together to create a life long master plan for your relationship.

## The Mastermind Treasure Hunt
### What would you like to work on first?

Financial
Health
Work
Home
Cars
Travel
Education
Entertainment
Sex
Kids
Spiritual/Religion/Philosophy
Politics and Activism
Philanthropy
Birthdays, Celebrations, and Other Big Events
Chores
Family Care and Elder Care
Friends
Clothing
Hobbies
Pets and Animals
Volunteer
Time

Of course your list will *not* be "The Perfect Plan." Your ideas and goals will change! The idea is to get the information out of your head and heart and into the collective brain of the relationship so that both parties can support one another. Think of a sailing team on the open sea. Having a target location allows all of the team members to support the travels of the ship. Mastermind planning does not have to be a system reserved only for bank robbers and businesses; you can tailor the idea to your needs as a couple.

## Hints and Tips

Having done this with my husband I can share a few hints and tips for getting the work accomplished.

1. Do the work together
2. Do the work alone and share together
3. Have one person be the scribe and the other the idea person, switch places
4. Work outside
5. Work in a new environment, a coffee shop, in front of a fireplace at a hotel, at a picnic table in a public place, work at a library (access to information), go to the top of a hill or mountain
6. Bring snacks and drinks to the table
7. Agree to work for only 15-20 minute increments initially, work up to more time, but not to the point of exhaustion
8. Smile
9. Draw pictures for each other
10. Record on video or voice
11. Laugh often
12. Collaborate

Ok, here we go! Let the list begin. You can start here at finance or you can start with travel or kids or whatever, it's up to you! But please, do the work. Without a plan, life will take you for the ride. With a plan, you create your own adventures.

## Financial

Do you remember my mother's sound advice? The three C's: Communication, Collaboration, and Cash? Directly and indirectly we have worked on the first two of the three C's — communication and collaboration. We have not talked a lot about the third C, Cash, yet. This is a section I would rather not include (people seem to carry so much baggage around money), but well, cash is ultra important, so I will add it and I hope you take a look at your financial situation.

So here it is, cash is really important. How are you going to handle your money? Don't tell me, talk to your partner. Oh, and by the way, I included a whole chapter on tracking, planning, and utilizing cash, it is the next chapter called: Fill In the Numbers. So start thinking about money a little bit while you complete the questions in this chapter, not just this section. Jot money notes down whenever they come to.

Take Action. With your partner, talk numbers, often and in detail. As with so many things in life, what you pay attention to improves, what you ignore festers. Allow your financial situation to grow and support your dreams by paying attention to the pennies.

List in your notebook, or better yet on your calendar, how often you plan to talk about money. Will you meet once a week, each month, quarterly, and/or yearly? Also, list how much detail you will cover at each meeting. Did I just say that? Am I asking you to make dates to talk about money? Yes I am, and yes you need to do this if you want to see valuable progress towards financial goals.

As I mentioned, at the end of the Mastermind chapter I will have an additional chapter to capture more detail on cash called: Fill In the Numbers. Right now, concentrate on finances at the global level within your relationship. When it feels appropriate jot down how much you spend in each section of the Mastermind Planning Sections go ahead and do so, and it is ok to guess at this point, you're getting your ideas on paper. Your actual numbers can be finessed in the next chapter.

Discuss enough vs. plenty. How much? His? Hers? Investments? Know the difference between active and passive income. List all income together; know where the accounts are and what the passwords are. Take your head out of the sand and pay attention to what is important — cash is king! Credit is only to be used sparingly and with wise council.

What kind of accounts do you have and what kinds do you want? Make a list: joint accounts, separate accounts, others (children, elder adults). Will both of you pay the bills or will one person have primary responsibility for all bill paying? If you split the responsibility how will you help each other to be accountable?

Cash In the Bank — When I was about 40 I was reading the book *Smart Women Finish Rich* by David Bach and I decided then and there that I wanted to be a millionaire before age 55. A lofty goal indeed! I told my husband and I told our financial advisor whom we had recently hired, because I was reading the book. Reaching tough goals is about soliciting support and help, even when you might want to keep the dream to yourself. Reaching a goal of this magnitude meant that someone, including myself, needed to believe it was possible. When my financial advisor did not laugh at me, but instead believed in us, I felt the strength of the possibility of making it happen growing.

You might be wondering...did we reach my goal? No, I am not 55 yet so I do not have an answer for you. Even if I did, the point is not how much, but that I dared to dream and I sought expert help and partner buy-in. And yes, we have worked towards the dream.

Do you have a cash dream? What is the amount and when do you want it by? Do you need the cash to be in liquid assets or non-liquid assets? Do you know the difference between these different types of assets?

**STOP: Time to take some notes!**

If your financial dreams are wildly different from your partner's, how can you bridge the gap?

Stock — buy, sell, hold, give away, discuss all transactions or do you decide to each have a private "play" account? Doesn't matter how you hold your stock accounts, what matters is that you both agree to what it means to have or not have stock shares.

What kind of stock? How much stock? Do you want to hold national investments or international investments? Will you get brokerage help or use on-line resources?

Bonds and other investment strategies, what are they and where are they held? Mutual funds and other investments, what are they, do you have them, do you want them?

Is it ok to cheat on your taxes? If so, how far do you push the envelope? If not, why not? What does it mean, actually, "to cheat" on taxes?

Home Purchase or Rent — this choice is very personal and will very likely bring up childhood issues and concerns. Take the time to listen to one another. While the American Dream has been for years: "To own a home." This may not be the best financial decision for your situation. The housing crash of 2008 changed the owners' market for the foreseeable future. I would recommend that you DO NOT assume that you cannot own a home, and conversely DO NOT assume that you must own a home. Seek counsel and work towards your *real* dreams.

My husband and I have both rented and owned property at different times in our marriage; both scenarios have pluses and minuses. Each decision was based on what would support the goals and our dreams as a couple and as a family. Every year was different. We are grateful that in America we can pursue different courses in life and we have varied housing choices.

This section, especially for homeowners, is best looked at in terms of a 5 or more year plan and out. Rarely, if ever does it pay to buy and sell a home sooner than the 5-year mark, 7 or more years is even is better. Unfortunately, I have learned this the hard way, through experience.

How about using real estate purchase for investment purposes? Would you choose individual home(s) or commercial property? Can you imagine yourself as a real estate investor? Why or why not?

Life Insurance — Whole versus Term, learn the difference and learn how to define these terms in your own words. Decide what you want or don't need. Put plans and meetings into place to make life insurance exist in your portfolio.

Trust Funds/Creating Trusts. Do you have a trust? Do you want or need a trust fund? What does it mean to you to have that money? What does it mean to you to prepare in this way for the future? Do you want to have a trust set up for your children or grandchildren? Seek professional assistance.

Entrepreneurial Endeavors — Owning a business or buying a business, is this even in the plan? Why or why not? Are you an entrepreneur? Do you already own your own business or businesses? Important because oftentimes immense amounts of money is spent on startups and the investment in new business ideas does not guarantee a re-coop of investment. On the other hand, entrepreneurial adventures can often reap far greater financial benefit than traditional nine-to-fiver jobs. What is the financial threshold that the parties in your relationship can withstand?

Creating a Will? Call a lawyer. Renew it every 5 years or less. Put a health clause in there. Make your dying wishes known. Be clear and concise. Explain exactly were your money is and where is should go after death. Who will make the phone call to initiate a meeting with a lawyer? When is the first meeting? What information has the lawyer asked you to gather? Do the work.

Once you have a grasp on your financial situation, come back and we will meander through issues of health.

## Health

What do you believe to be more important, health or finances?

Trick question.

As long as you are alive these two life issues are integral to everyday existence. My belief is that the United States of America is in a health care vortex of trouble. Too many people are obese, in danger of serious health problems, or living with health issues that could have been avoided. To add insult to injury, good healthcare and preparing healthy food is extraordinarily expensive — in time and money. Many people claim that eating healthier is more expensive, but I have found the opposite to be true. Purchasing whole foods, bringing them home, preparing meals, cleaning after cooking from scratch, and planning ahead to have healthful meals takes far more expenditure of time than money. Yet still, I will try to prevail and cook whole foods, eat less, and stay healthy!

A while ago, one of my sons was diagnosed as being in the obese category on US health charts. I was not far behind at 188+ pounds and 5'8" tall. This was a terrible time. I felt like I had failed at a key component in my mastermind family planning goals. I had failed to recognize and listen to my own body. I had failed my son, but I was not sure how. I had failed to pay attention to my health. I woke up. I made enormous changes in *my* diet and in *my* fitness routine. Since then, I have been actively seeking health care professionals and fitness professionals to aid me on my road to recovering my own health on many levels, not only my weight.

I am not going to tell you that this was or is easy for me. Loosing weight, learning to eat differently, and taking care of my health has been one of the hardest things I have focused on in the past few years. At this time, I have not accomplished my goals for myself, yet. I struggle daily with wanting food that I know does not sustain my health. I continue to have off-moments when I eat the poison that I know will make me feel physically awful in a few minutes, a few hours, or even the next day. I am sure you know what your poison is, we all have our vices. Also, I might add that the more I cleaned up my diet the more I learned what foods I could tolerate and what foods make me feel ill. This is an on-going process of discovery and learning.

Fitness together is FUN!

Enough about that! No, actually I have a bit more to say. Just over 2 years ago my husband had stopped eating at regular intervals. Yes, he stopped eating! I did not even notice (in my defense, he is at work much of the time)! He lost a ton of weight and he nearly slipped into Type 2, Adult Onset Diabetes! I thought this could only happen to people who are overweight. Not true. His liver could not figure out how to regulate his sugar levels because he was eating so irregularly! This was a scary time for us. Luckily, due to our goal of visiting a doctor once per year no matter what, the blood test caught what he and I had failed to take notice of. Do not put off seeing the doctor, once a year at minimum. Preventative healthcare is far less expensive than illness.

I cannot make my son eat less or differently, that was and is his job. He puts the food on his own plate and makes his own choices (especially since he is away at school for much of the year). However, that did not stop me from commenting on his food choices while we were at meals together (this angers him though, and makes things worse, so I have learned to stop). I could not force feed my husband and make sure that he would eat — but I sure wanted to. In the end, I realize I could only change *me*! I could only be supportive, instead of controlling. I could only make sure that the food provided in our home was whole foods, healthy and nutritious choices. This essentially means that I bring home tons of vegetables, fruits, nuts, and whole grains with meat and poultry served sparingly, if at all.

Are you picking up on the labyrinth that lay in our household for family meal planning? Two of us had to eat far less, and one of us had to start eating far more and more importantly, more often! The fourth amongst us seemed to have figured out his own eating, but he too had other health daemons to contend with. I was the person who had to "chill out!" Family members who I loved dearly had to each find their own path to wellness. I was once again learning that I could not control those I love...

> *None of us can control the behaviors of others; we can only take notice of our own behaviors and reactions.*

Going through these health events woke me up to the importance of excellent health. Of course, I always knew it, but now the issue was In My Face! Here is the reality: We can 100% take control of our own health. Sadly, we cannot ensure the health of those we love. However, I believe that couples can influence one another's behaviors both positively and negatively. This Mastermind section is about gaining clarity on how much time, energy, and money you will spend on good health as individuals, as a couple, and if you have children, as a family.

Healthcare for the sick is so expensive that I constantly worry that in the future healthcare will determine people's quality of life more so even than home ownership or cash in the bank. This is in fact already starting to happen for many people and families. We have been ignoring for too long the real costs of ill health. I do hope that this section captures your full attention and time. Good Luck!

Take Action. Be specific in your responses here!

Weight — discuss ideal vs. reality, discuss what commitments you will take to get to where you want to be. Conversely, is weight simply not an issue at all... because in your estimation, life is meant for living it up! Eat, drink, and be merry! Do you believe that your weight can change for the better permanently or are you content with where you are? Are you ready to take on the emotional and social challenge of what it means to loose weight and keep it off?

Food Consumption and Choices — who shops, who cooks, where do you shop? What is the budget? What are some "hang-ups" in this realm? For example, my family does not want me to become a "hippy-health-nut" — yet in many ways I already am. Also, I live with a family member who will not eat fish, nor does this person want me to even cook fish when they are around and I love fish!

*STOP: Time to take some notes!*

Pills/pharmaceuticals/naturopathic remedies/essential oils/supplements — what are your beliefs around this? Some people believe that pharmaceuticals are not necessary and that diet alone can cure, others believe in massive use of dietary supplements and pharmaceuticals. Where are you on the continuum? Where is your partner? Do your views agree or clash? Can there be a middle ground? How? How will medically necessary pharmaceuticals be paid for?

Alcohol consumption — How much is enough? How often? What kind of alcohol is acceptable or unacceptable? What is the "breaking point" of too much drinking? How much money is spent on this optional item? Or is alcohol considered a necessity in your lifestyle? Conversely, is alcohol taboo for medical, religious or other reasons?

Recreational drugs — Do you condone or condemn the use of recreational drugs? Which drugs? How much is enough? How often? What is the "breaking point" of too much use of these elective additives to your diet and life-style? How much money is spent on this inessential item? Conversely, are recreational drugs considered a necessity in your lifestyle? Or, are recreational drugs taboos for legal, medical, religious or other reasons?

Teeth — Do you go to the dentist twice a year? Do you brush twice a day for two minutes? Do you floss? Do you plan to do corrective treatment? Do you plan tooth enhancements such as whitening or veneers? What else would you consider important around the notion of having a great smile and healthy teeth?

protect your eyes

Eyes — Do you go to the eye doctor once a year? Do you get enough rest? Do you wear sunglasses and a hat to protect your eyes in bright sun? Do you plan to do corrective treatment or surgery? Do you wear corrective lenses or contacts? Are glasses a fashion statement or a necessity for seeing?

Other Body Parts — There are doctors today who can change your looks from head to toe. Literally. Facelifts, nose jobs, boob jobs, stomach reduction, hip minimizing, labia beautification, penis enlargement, scrotum lift, foot reconfiguration (yes, people have their feet altered so that they can fit into pointier high heeled shoes or so that they can run long distances and not have toenail trouble, and other elective procedures as well), and many other body parts can be altered to suit the needs of the individual or the couple's enjoyment of one another. Have you ever asked each other how you feel about these elective surgeries and procedures? Discuss how much alteration is enough. Discuss the annual budget for these alterations. Discuss if you think this should not be in the health section of this book, but as some other category.

Body Piercing, Tattoos and other body alterations — I am not an expert in this area at all. However, I have attempted as much as possible to stay informed. I have asked people questions about their personal enhancements — yes, I do simply say things like, "How do you add those earrings into your earlobe, how does it work?" Additionally, I have watched many documentaries on the topic of body alterations. Yet, I have double ear piercings, and that's it, a naked body!

Still, I believe one should take the time to talk about these commonplace and nearly-socially acceptable body enhancements (there are some people who call enhancements atrocities, I know this and you know this, let's stay open minded). While I am at it, sadly, "socially acceptable" is a broad swath of untruth, there are still so many areas in our society were tattoos are considered to be: "the wrong message," "sad," "unacceptable," or phrased another way, "un-hirable." I have even heard that judges in a court of law continue to make decisions about ones ability to pay court fines based on how many visible tattoos there are: the argument being if you have enough money for tattoos, you will have enough money to pay your fines! This is unfair, but the discrimination exists.

I say, for the purposes of your increased understanding of one another, have the conversation. There is much more to this topic that I am completely naïve about, I realize this, but the topic is worth your consideration. How does each of you feel about the addition of body piercing, tattoos, and other body alterations on each other and in society in general? Is there an age limit, for example, do you believe it is acceptable for children to ask for and get tattoos and other body enhancements? When children get tattoos and body enhancements who pays for it, the child, the parent, or someone else? Some tattoos are used in place of makeup...the potential is endless. The point is to please go ahead and have the honest and truthful conversations. Listen to each other with kindness and learn from other as much as possible.

Years ago I took our family to a large tattoo expo so that we could have first hand experience of the culture around tattoos and body enhancements. Visiting the expo was no different from a field trip to a museum, zoo, street art fair, or RV expo. I looked at it as just another life experience and a chance to learn. We spent hours asking questions while we were there and talking to one another about what we learned from being at the expo.

*STOP: Time to take some notes!*

Active Physical Activities — Active physical activities are good for your health, some however can lead to injury and even death. What will you bring to your relationship? What activities do you want to do alone? Which activities would you like to participate in as a couple? I could not possibly list for you all of the incredible physical activities available for you to try. All sorts of choices exist from extreme sports and events, to gentle floor stretching, and everything in between. My husband does kite boarding, half marathons, and Spartan Races (a form of extreme running and boot camp race at top speed). He has also jumped out of an airplane for the fun of it! I, on the other hand, participate in yoga, outdoor fitness classes, swimming, and walking. Clearly my speed is slower than his! When we first met we used to bike together, rollerblade, and hike regularly. Now we tend to try to find a happy middle — often this means walking or biking, and once in a while kayaking. Find what works for you, and even if you do not participate in activities as a couple, stay active.

Fitness: A walk is all it takes!

I should mention here, that my pace of fitness has slowed down exponentially due to early onset of osteoarthritis. I was diagnosed at age 39. I deal with chronic pain. There have been months that I can only walk a mile at a time at what I call my zen speed, I consciously take each step slowly to minimize the impact of pain in my knees. Failing this, I go swimming instead. I also know there are steps I can take to reduce the pain and avoid painkillers; for example diet and physical therapy.

I dearly miss being able to run and move fast, but if I want to keep the pain at bay, I must listen to the signals my body is sending me on a daily basis and sometimes hourly. I have managed to keep the disease at: "mild degenerative" levels for ten years (as diagnosed by experts via x-rays). That's not to say that some months or days are not hellish, but with proper stretching, rest, ice, heat, diet, and appropriate activities I can usually get the pain under control in a few days, although sometimes it takes weeks. If you are dealing with any healthcare issues that are on going, I urge you to take better care of yourself. When my pain is under control, everything else in life is much more pleasant. I would like this for you.

I also need to add that with the recent health changes that I made for myself I have actually been able to do some running for a little over a month now. I never expected to be able to move at a running speed ever again. Change can happen. I am enjoying the feeling of moving faster. At the same time I know that the inflammation of arthritis could return and worsen again. I am grateful for the change I have found in my body and I smile while I run.

What do you do to learn more about health? I tend to read books, watch movies, and seek personal counsel from experts. Learning more about the topic of health is really important to me. I beg you, do not take your health for granted!

I have said this before in the finance section of Mastermind Planning, but it bears repeating: pay attention to what you pay attention to! You reap what you sew. If you need further information on how to maintain your optimal health, then by all means seek expert advice from doctors and people you trust. Be super wary and careful about media reports, often they are incorrect.

Take Action. List books, movies, and people you wish to learn more from. Do you want to learn more together? Is doing the work of health research by yourself enough? Schedule times on your calendar to follow through on taking action.

*STOP: Time to take some notes!*

For you, what does it mean to be stress free? Is this possible? If it is possible, how do you plan to arrive at a stress free life? Is stress good for you, if so when is stress helpful? Know your top three stress triggers; share them with your partner.

Let's consider doctor visits and different types of doctors and health care practitioners. Some people never visit a doctor — unless there is a dire emergency! Other people visit the doctor once a year, and still others go once a week or more. Talk about this and what the decision you make for your body means to you. Talk about the many kinds of doctors and practitioners there are such as: Acupuncture, Chiropractic, Acupressure, Nutritionist, Massage Therapist, Herbalist, and many others.

What are some other types of practitioners that you can think of? When would you use their services? What services do you think are a hoax and should never be considered for optimal health?

*STOP: Time to take some notes!*

All of the above Health components take considerable amounts of money and time to maintain. Adding and subtracting health services and products will be in flux during your lifetime in part due to your lifestyle. Currently, what do you spend in time and money for healthcare expenditures? Do you have health insurance? If not, why not?

Other aspects of healthcare are: make-up, healthcare products, beauty products and personal care products. Keep track for a few days. What do you use? How much? Do you consider the health risks to products with chemicals? Do you use unscented and chemical free products? Why? Have you ever considered the products you use as being a part of your healthcare regimen? Do you consider the products you use and their impact on our environment?

Write the figures down such as money spent and the time spent per week, month, per year — consider everything related to health. Insurance. Food. Alcohol. Recreational drugs. Healthcare providers, alternative health care practitioners, and healthcare products. Fitness centers. Fitness trainers. Eyewear and dentist appointments and even elective teeth procedures (braces, whitening, caps, veneers). Include in your expenditures sports, sporting equipment, events and other activity or health fees and travel. Dream about and consider how much you wish you could spend. Pull back and think about what is the least amount you could spend. Write down ideas of what life would look like if a minimal amount of cash was spent on health-related costs. Can you and your partner collaborate on a "best case scenario?" Interestingly, when I did this with my husband we realized we spend a larger portion of our income on health related expenses than we thought we did! We have since made some adjustments. How about you, what can you learn from tracking all spending related to health?

*STOP: Time to take some notes!*

How long do you want to live? Maybe this question should be put first under health, because it will dictate many of the above choices. Still, a worthwhile conversation, if you plan to live to be 100, what do you do *now* to ensure an excellent future quality of life? If you'd rather die young doing what you love, your partner deserves to know and understand your viewpoint and action plan. Talk about how long you plan to live.

Embedded in this question is another one worth addressing. Whose responsibility is your health? I cannot tell you how many times I hear people sitting at the doctors office or in another public space saying: "My doctor can't figure it out, I don't know what's wrong with me…" Guess what? In many instances the doctor will never figure it out! *Taking care of your body is your responsibility.* Make it a priority always, but even more so when you don't feel well.

Keep in mind that medical doctors may not be in the practice of asking you about your diet and habits; they are primarily concerned with dispensing the best pharmaceuticals. This is not wrong; it is the way our system currently operates. Don't blame your doctor! Only you know what you are doing and putting into your body that is causing ill health. Get real. Get honest and most of all listen to your body, it has the answers you need if you take the time to listen. Yes, I know what you are thinking, sometimes the answer does come from a doctor, but honestly I believe many of our health issues are due to our own bad habits!

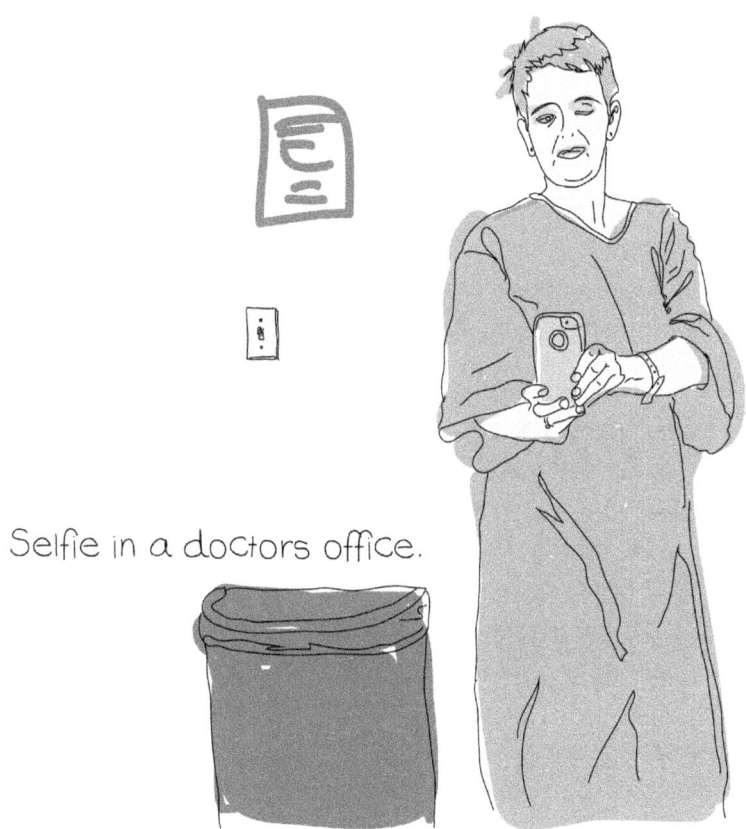

Selfie in a doctors office.

Get Real. What health habits do you practice that you know are contributing negatively to your daily life and overall wellbeing? What habits do you know could add to your feeling better, but you somehow do not manage to "find the time or money?"

*STOP: Time to take some notes!*

Typically we choose to work to stay healthy so that we can earn a living, spend quality time with family, and do the stuff we love. The next section explores work habits and realities.

## Work

In my adult life, the actual years I have spent working for someone else outside the home has been about 8 total. Most of my adult life I have been a free agent and self-employed or a full-time wife and mother. When I work I tend to either work on a contractual basis, as a landlord, as a teacher, or I sell my art and creative endeavors. I have even sold my stuff when I needed cash for a project that was important to me.

For much of my adult life, I balanced motherhood with the most minimal amount of paid work for organizations outside the home as I could get away with. Not because I don't like to work, conversely, I work long hours that often feel like I do all-of-the-time-working. The difference is, for me, work is defined in broad terms. Laundry is work. Cooking is work. Writing this book is work. Maintaining the household calendar is work. Marketing and building my website is work. Life is work. Work, as in a j-o-b, for me is what I fit around my real life's work. For many, serial contractual work is not a model of success. I understand that. I am supremely grateful for the choices I have been able to maintain. Yet, I also complain regularly that the balance of work is off-kilter in our relationship, but that's a whole other book! I am learning to tune into my complaining and make changes, and I believe you can too.

In this section I am asking you to ask yourself, what do you want your work life or work/life to look like?

By getting clear on what work means to you and your partner you may find the right fit for happiness, flexibility, stability, and income. I believe that the future of work and jobs is drastically changing to new models due in large part to the way work is conducted via the Internet. By the time my children find adult level work, I do not think the same percentage of jobs will be done in the model of: "having a job at an organization." Future generations will need to be able to travel to where the work is, they will need to know exactly what skills, talents, and passions they have to offer to others and to organizations. It will be their job to re-train and re-educate themselves regularly because corporations are not going to keep spending money on these activities. They will simply "go elsewhere" and find qualified trained individuals to meet their needs. Most importantly, people will need exemplary collaborative and self-marketing skills in order to earn a living.

I often think that I would like a stable income, like the regular paycheck that comes from a 9 to 5er job. However, that leap would take changes that at this time I cannot see or do not recognize as a possibility for me. I have lived through my adult life following my passions, my mission, and vision. I have always made sure that I pay myself (ourselves) first (IRA, husband's 401(k), and savings for a "rainy day." Then the bills get paid on time every time (well, not exactly, we are all human). We have never purchased a vacation on credit. We have learned to pay off our car loans in two years (in most cases) and we keep our cars for as long as possible once we own them. I could go on, but my point is that we spend what we have not what we think we will get in the future. Working to live vs. living to work — you need to decide your goals.

I am very fortunate to have fallen in love with a man who values stability rather than the flexibility that I value. We make our work life work for us. Like many people, we often desire more money, but when we look close at what we have accomplished with what we have as a couple and align our hopes, goals, and dreams with how much we do have, we try to make sure that work does not ruin our life. This balance is very difficult to come by and we constantly search for better solutions. The work we do supports who we are as a couple. Usually we realize that we do have enough — money that is. Time is another issue entirely.

I hope that Mastermind Planning in the area of work can help you to clarify what you want your work pattern to look like. Be open to doing the work it takes to do what works for you in the area of work. How's that for a tongue twister!

Take Action. Think and talk about these questions: What age will you work until? Will you work for others or be self-employed? Do you plan to travel for work or not? Are there anticipated changes in current employment or a plan stay the course? What makes you happy at work? Why do you work? What is it beyond the paycheck that drives you? Is retirement a word in your vocabulary or do you plan to work your whole life?

**STOP: *Time to take some notes!***

The bigger question here is building awareness of how your personal Passion, Mission, and Vision are supported in how you spend your time at work and in life's pursuits.

Take the idea of developing a Passion, Mission, and Vision (Chapter 11) for yourselves and as a couple. Write initial ideas down and realize that adjustments will need to be made over time.

## Home

For me, "Home" is a concept that I long to understand. By the age of 13, I had lived in 11 different homes. Now at the age of 49 I can claim 38 different addresses as "my home" or places I have lived, slept, and made memories. My son who is 15 has lived at 13 different addresses. As I write this, I dream of building a custom home one day and living in it for the rest of my life. Except there are so many things I love about all of the places that I have lived in that in all honestly I am not sure I would be able to envision what my "one true best place" to live in would look and feel like. As I said, I long to understand the concept of "home." For now, home is wherever I am, I guess!

My husband spent his childhood in two different homes. The one he was born in and the one he moved into at age eight. Then he went to college, graduated, moved back in with his mother and moved in with me. His mother still lives in the second home he grew up in. His concept of home has been shattered while living with me. Like us, you and your partner my have gloriously different concepts of home.

Take Action. Where will you live? Some people buy one house and stay put, regardless of job satisfaction and family changes. Others move too much and too often. Do you live exactly as you wish and in the best place possible for you as a couple? If so, what is it that you are so grateful for? Write down all the details. Do you long for something else? If so, what? Research your thoughts and write down the details. Below I will get you started with possible considerations.

Single-Family Home, Multi-Family Dwelling, Apartment, Mobile Home, Boat/RV/Tent, size in square feet, number of bathrooms, bedrooms, pool, fireplace, den, view, new, old. Kind of home: Spanish style, adobe, modern, Victorian, IKEA, mid-century modern, Tudor, loft, manufactured, or other? Maybe none of this stuff means home, if so what does?

*STOP: Time to take some notes!*

Next consider the location of home where you would like to build your relationship: city, country, suburb, new, historic district, lake, forest, river, ocean, sea, or mountain. Use detail to describe your ideal space to live. Take into consideration job satisfaction, hobbies, like minded people, services and amenities you require, sporting activities, culture and so on... Exhaust the possibilities of what most interests you in terms of lifestyle and comfort. Maybe for you, location has only one variable, your proximity to extended family members.

Let's take home and money. What percent of income you wish to spend as a couple towards rent/mortgage, taxes and insurance? Bank loans vary from 15% - 33%, but before you borrow, learn what is best for you, not what the bank thinks is best. What is your, "I sleep like a baby at night," number? How do you plan to maintain that threshold?

Do you want to own one, two, three homes or more? Do you wish to own more than one home at a time and have one as a vacation dwelling? How about a Recreational Vehicle or Boat as a home? What kinds of homes have I failed to mention as viable living situations? How do these alternative types of living arrangements support your vision for your partnership? Is the nomad lifestyle more to your liking?

Take Action. Think about the future. While we are on the topic of home, take a moment to jot down your expectations for yourself and for each of you within the relationship in the area of active living for seniors, assisted living, and other later-in-life living situations. What do you think you want and why? Remember, you can change your mind, but by taking a moment to discuss the options this conversation will come as less of a surprise when you are approaching the "nearly-dead" phase of your relationship.

*STOP: Time to take some notes!*

Homes are often one of our biggest and most expensive purchases, next up is car ownership.

## Cars

How many cars do you think you will own in your lifetime? Will the number be 8 or 30 or more? Seriously. A new car every 5 years equals about 8 new-to-you cars in your lifetime. Do you want a new car every other year? Then expect to own about 30 cars. With cars (not including trucks or luxury vehicles) weighing in at a median range of $25,000 to $35,000 in 2014, that is a big chunk of change! Recent studies are pointing out that the average American is spending more on a car than they can afford. This is a catch-22, you need a car for work and you work to pay off cars that are becoming more and more expensive to own.

You cannot afford *not* to talk about cars. Cars are the third biggest expense after home and health care, I think, depending on your vacation spending and clothing, food and entertainment budgets. Anyway, you get the idea, every few years you and your partner will need to discuss cars.

I can tell you, car conversations have always created friction in our household. He wants a fast-customized sports car. I want him to drive the practical large car. I want a small zippy car. He wants me to drive the family-sized car. Every 5 to 7 years we go through the same long drawn out discussions. We communicate, collaborate, and compromise. Yes, this is one area where compromise has always needed to happen.

I know people who replace their car every two years. I know people who own several vintage or collectible cars. I know people who share one car, and one motorcycle. I also know people who have a car that barely runs, but that is all that they can afford, and they end up occasionally missing out on appointments and opportunities because their car is once again "in the shop."

You will need to ask yourselves and each other where car ownership falls on your continuum of life values and importance. Ask yourselves, new shoes or being able to afford the car payment? New fishing gear or car payment? You see where this conversation can get ticklish, don't you?

Take Action. Here are some questions to continue the conversation.

**STOP: Time to take some notes!**

How many cars do you expect to own at one time? What kind of cars? What, when, how do you plan to replace used and or non-drivable cars? What do you plan to do with non-drivable cars? Do you keep them or dump them? How often would you, ideally, like to replace your car? How do you plan to pay for car replacement needs? Savings, cash, or loans? Do you plan on buying cars for the kids or not? Are there any car brands that land on the NO WAY YOU CANNOT BUY THAT TYPE OF CAR list? May as well get this detail out in the open!

Possibly, you do not want a car at all? You'd rather live in a city such as NYC that requires no car and provides excellent public transportation. What if you are one of those people that would love to fly to work! Yes, there are communities that have small aircraft garages instead of, or in addition to, car garages. Maybe you would you prefer a full-time chauffer? Ah, let's move on to travel.

## Travel

Travel not only expands your knowledge base it also disrupts the usual flow of life. I adore travel, and I hate airports! I love going to places where I do not have to do any driving during my visit. Without regular travel planned each year I have found that I get anxious and even depressed. Sometimes so much so that I feel like I need to move into another home! My husband does not seem to require travel plans in his life as much as I do, so I go alone to places. What might work for you?

Take Action. There are at least three types of travel: Vacations, Work Travel, and Family Visit Travel. Jot down how many days, weeks or months you believe you will be spending away from home and traveling each year.

*STOP: Time to take some notes!*

Will the travel be near and far? Where to? How often? Are there a few places that you must visit and see before you die? What distant locations are they? List some detail around the "must-do" trip.

Whose family do you visit on the holidays? What holidays are used for visiting family? Are there people in your life that are not family, but they are treated as such and need to be included in this conversation? How often do you visit family?

Ok so here is the question that may start the giggles or a seriously frustrating conversation – who tends to pack too much? Who knows how to bring the right amount of stuff? Who brings enough to move-in to your new location? Does one of you love luggage and the idea of travel and has too much luggage but hardly any stamps in his or her passport?

Oh, while we are on the subject of passports, do you both have one? Do you wish you had one? Do either of you have dreams of travelling to an exotic, historic, or some other "bucket list" place? What is stopping you from beginning to set plans for visiting? Do you dream of a trip around the world? Do you dream of visiting every continent? What travel dream do you have that you keep deeply hidden for fear of never being able to make it happen? Get it out in the open, enlist support in following your dreams.

How often do you travel alone? How often do you travel as a couple? How often do you travel as a family? When you travel do you expect to travel budget style, first class, or something in-between? Do you dream of owning a share of private jet or maybe even your own jet?

Do you believe in the idea of stay-cations? If so, who does the cleaning, housework, food preparation and local area trip planning while vacationing from home? Do you plan to own or rent a recreational vehicle or boat for travel fun?

What distance equals a need for a hotel for the night? For example, I regularly travel by car over 200 miles in a single day, roundtrip, to spend time with my children. Other people may find that a hotel is required for that travel distance. Only you know your limits.

Is there a place that your family returns to time and time again, but your enjoyment of the place has worn thin? What alternate situation could be made? If you love the place you visit every year, have you considered making it a permanent residence or purchasing a second home?

Travel is a form of world knowledge or education, next we will look at traditional education models.

## Education

In my family, education has always been highly valued. The same is true for my husband's family. One might say we took this value to the extreme; we both have two master's degrees. We love the campus experience. I often dream of earning a PhD that deals with human issues, communication and art (if that degree exists). The land of college and university campuses is not the best place for everyone though. Furthermore, education comes in many forms. Trade schools, online classes, retreats, conferences, and world travel all count as education.

Take Action. What education do you already have and what more do you want to learn? Do you value education that does not lead to employment? Is learning for the sake of learning a valued use of time and resources? Why or why not?

*STOP: Time to take some notes!*

New skills. Are there new things you want to learn? Would you like to: fly an airplane, learn ballroom dancing, pick up knitting, or scuba diving? Dream a little or a lot. What new skill would you love to add to your life's path? You might find a skill that you both want to learn together, how cool would that be!

More degrees. Would a new degree help or hinder your progress in the workplace? If further education would be of great value at work or in your life what is stopping you? How can you burst through your blocks and go for it? Have you, like me, ever dreamed of holding a PhD?

Certificates and licenses are other forms of further education. There are many avenues for second incomes that can become a reality through certificate or licensure training and education. For example, yoga, electrician, plumber, coach, notary public, organization specialist, Pilates instructor and others. Have you had a nagging desire to do more with your life, and offer skills you love to use that may take only 6 to 18 months to accomplish? Can you find the money to fund your education? Can you make the time? How? Why have you been holding yourself back? Write down a plan to move forward with a dream.

Teach others. Sometimes further education means that you share what you already know with others. How about writing a course proposal to a community college, adult school, or senior center? How about making your own on-line class. If you do long to share your wealth of knowledge to educate others what would you teach? Where or who can you propose your course ideas to?

*STOP: Time to take more notes!*

Give back. This is similar to above, but giving back could be in the form of becoming a board member or volunteer at a place of higher education, a museum, or some other non-profit that places a value on education (Scouting, FIRST, Boys & Girls Clubs and others). Where would you love to serve? How can you meet the people with the power to add you to the roster of potential service?

Do you plan on spending time on retreats as a form of education, job or life enrichment? Does your partner consider retreats to be "vacation"? How is educational retreat time different from vacation time? Have the conversation and get clear with one another. What other types of educational experiences did I inadvertently leave out of the equation that may be important to you?

How does education differ and how is it similar to entertainment? Next topic is entertainment.

## Entertainment

Concerts, movies, amusement parks, museums, sporting events, books, plays, ballet...and the all-important season tickets!

Relax with a book.

Take Action. Write down your current customary entertainment avenues. Then dream a little or a lot and write down your biggest most dreamy entertainment scenarios. Think big here. Do you go to the Olympics with first class seats? Do you attend the soccer World Cup? Do you travel to Japan to see world-class Japanese drummers? Quite a lot of entertainment ideas might also be addressed in another section of the Mastermind chapter. Have fun entertaining the idea of an entertaining life!

*STOP: Time to take more notes!*

I am an avid reader. Reading is quite possibly my favorite form of entertainment. About three months into my marriage, a long time ago... my husband announced: "Honey, you're banned from book buying. Go to the library!" While his method lacked in finesse, kindness, and overall effectiveness — it did not go unnoticed. I still buy books with alarming regularity, including electronic books and audio books. However, I also do use the library with gusto! How can you stretch your entertainment budget? Is sex entertainment?

## Sex

I expect you to hash out the details of your sex life in your own way with the help of other coaches, teachers, writers and film directors. However, having said that, I also want you to dream in this realm as well. Dream and talk about your dreams. Dream and listen to your partners' dreams.

> *There's so much more to sex, love and relationships than fitting a specific peg in one specific hole.* — Julianne Ross

My sex life is private. I have no details to share here. Yeah, I know, you bought this book to read these details — Ha, not really! Seriously though, one's own journey on the path to a satisfying loving relationship and sex life is what we're looking at here. I want you to ask each other questions, and communicate about this chapter section without words.

Take Action. A very special way to approach this chapter is to set aside one hour no talking session. Explore through smell, sight, touch, taste, and listening. Consider the use of a safe word. Seriously, no talking! What could you learn from one another by being present with each other in the same space and not talking?

Did you know sexual intercourse typically lasts about 2 to 7 minutes? Crazy right! Orgasm lasts but a few brief seconds. That's what research says... Maybe you only have five minutes, great, then, go for it! But for more fulfilling and cherished encounters consider the millions of other ways, paths, and journeys to intimacy. Including setting aside more than 2 to 7 minutes of your time!

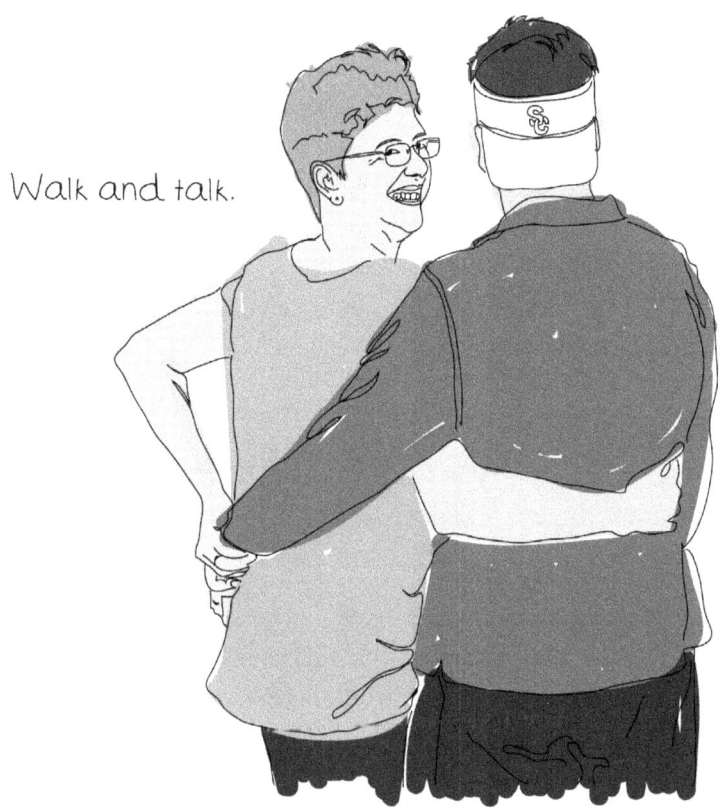

Walk and talk.

Take Action. Make sure you do whatever works for you and your partner, s-l-o-w-l-y! Ok, so you tried the one-hour of no talking, what's next? Get talking, of course! Since sex is often a touchy subject I suggest you set a timer for say, 20 minutes and each of you fill out some answers to these questions alone, then bring the responses together in a kind and generous way. What does that mean?

1. Look each other in the eye.
2. Hold hands.
3. Never laugh, well I hate the word never, but you know what I mean...we are talking about respecting each other's viewpoints, ideas, and requests.

Need some help getting into the mood? What is your favorite romantic movie? Have you visited a sex store together? I mean a good one with an excellent reputation; well ok, go to a seedy one too, why not? Have you ever kidnapped your partner and brought them to a sensual place, like an ocean cottage or a mountain hut for a weekend? If not, why not? Have you explored products that can aid couples in enhanced sexual positions? Have you ever offered a back rub or foot rub expecting absolutely nothing in return, if not why not?

**STOP: Time to take some notes!**

How much sex? What kind? Where? When? How often is enough? How vanilla or risqué? Drugs, toys, massage? Locations? Mile high club? Beach? Under a tree? On a boat?

What about encounters beyond the relationship? Is this ok or would this mean death of the relationship? Is self-pleasure a topic up for discussion? Masturbation? Vibrators? Dildos?

Take Action. What if asking questions really does not appeal to you in regards to sex? Then don't ask each other these questions! However, you could try setting a 20 minute timer to talk about sex — with no touching, smelling, kissing, hugging, only talking. And by the way, force the talk to be about sex *only* for the full 20 minutes. Then decide what's next.

I will mention the two things that I know work better than anything else I can say to strengthen a relationship and can lead to more fulfilling sexual lives.

1. Practice.
2. Touch.

Consider the practice of kissing each other every single day, once in the morning, once at night, more as needed. Practice hugging each other daily and linger in the embrace often. Practice holding your loved ones hand whenever possible.

> *I blame my mother for my poor sex life. All she told me was 'the man goes on top and the woman underneath.' For three years my husband and I slept in bunk beds.* — Joan Rivers

Yeah, I know, I sound soooo darn vanilla and white breadish again! I warned you. But seriously, if you ask my brother and sister why they think that our parents have stayed happily married for 50 years, the one thing we can all agree on is the power of touch. My parents hold hands frequently, especially when taking walks together. My sister tells stories of my parents dancing in the kitchen joyfully before or after dinner. My brother sites all the foot rubs or neck rubs my father gave my mother in the evening in front of the TV in the family room amongst the chaos of a household with three children. They have been married fifty years and we still catch them touching, holding, and caring for one another on a regular basis!

> *If your sex life is not what you want it to be, start with the practice of touch.*

There are zillions of studies about the power of touch. There are studies about how touch can heal the pains of ageing adults. There are studies on premature babies miraculously gaining weight when the parents desperate to help their child thrive and grow spend a great deal of time touching their child amidst the tubes and machines. I can tell you from first-hand experience that my children who are teenage boys resist my touch, but they cave in and linger in a good embrace at least once daily. Touch is magical.

Umm, sex can lead to the next topic…kids!

## Kids

Let's be real here. Children cost a shitload of money. Yes, shitload — a whole great huge pile of stinkin' cash! They require a whole lot of money to support them from birth until...I am not sure when...forever? They also take precious time and energy away from a committed relationship. Honestly, they really do!

> *Children have a primal need to know who they are, to love and be loved by the two people whose physical union brought them here. To lose that connection, that sense of identity, is to experience a wound that no child-support check or fancy school can ever heal. — David Blankenhorn*

Children are not to be taken lightly, especially in our throw away society. By the way, maybe you are a grandparent reading this book, thanks! Dive in think about the following questions from the standpoint of a grandparent, sure many questions will be irrelevant, but many others are not. Maybe you are in a relationship and do not have children yet, but you might, someday. These questions are worth reviewing ahead of time. OK, now that I have gotten those statements about money and time off my chest and out of the way let's dive in!

Take Action. Do you want kids? I mean really want to raise kids all the way to adulthood and beyond. How much of a sacrifice are you really willing to make to be a good parent, and by that I mean, not a friend to your kids but a real parent. A person who sets boundaries, loves unconditionally, and acts like a parent.

> *You should consider for your children that if they and their future spouse experience parental divorce, the odds of divorce nearly triple. — Racheal Tasker*

How many children do you plan to parent? Does your number jive with your significant other? Have you talked about the possible discrepancy? He wants 7 and you want only one? What do you do? Maybe one or both of you does not want kids at all...

How much time would you ideally like to spend with them? Consider every age as best as you can.

How much financial support do you plan to dish out? Until what age will you continue to offer financial support? If you and your partner have different ideas around financially supporting adult children, go back to active listening and find a place of collaboration. Remember that committed relationships put each other first, or at least that is the goal.

Children come AS IS. You cannot pick "perfect" children. Actually, they are ALL perfect, but what I mean is, children come AS IS. You never know from day to day, month-to-month, or year-to-year what the challenges might be. Every moment really is precious and you never get to "go back" or have "do-overs" when raising your children. Please take this seriously, children are little miracles and need to be valued as such. In fact, there are times in a child's life when you do not even know how they are going to act from minute to minute — this is most noticeable in — toddlers or teenagers. The moments you get to spend with your children are special and magical.

Let go and let them be who they are. When you do, the relationship between you and them will develop more beautifully.

Take Action. If you have not yet had kids, or even if you have, consider taking about your biggest fears in the area of differently-abled children, children who are born with diseases that last a lifetime, or children that become very sick. Discuss also discipline, drug use, alcohol use, money, sex, and the millions of other scenarios of child rearing.

***STOP: Time to take some notes!***

My husband for example, worried endlessly and lost sleep over the possibility of my delivering a disabled child. For both pregnancies, he was a wreck of nerves. At times it made him irrational and irritable about the activities I could do or the foods I would eat. We never could have anticipated his extreme worry, but there it was, and that was before the children were even born! Be honest with each other and be kind, because like children, your partner comes AS IS.

*Remain committed to your family; children deserve our best.*

Sometimes the worst of the worst happens, and no amount of mastermind preparation can assist you in the journey called life with kids. Know this. Remember this and keep faith, patience, and forgiveness as top priorities.

Take Action. Yep, as in all these sections, here come the questions!

What are your deepest hopes for your children? What are your dreams for your kids? Do you have high expectations for their future or do you believe they create their own future after a certain age?

What role will religion play in raising your kids? What kind of education do you expect to provide? Are sports mandatory? Music lessons? Dance? Tutors for academics? Therapists? Braces for perfect teeth? Brand new clothes or hand me downs? Do you make decisions together or defer to one parent? Do you have expectations for high grades, friends, and other life choices?

College Funds — will you pay for college or is that your children's responsibility? Because at college age they are already an adult after all...

*STOP: Time to take some notes!*

Are your children permitted to keep living at home after the age of 18? How about after 21, 25, or 35? Will they need to be cared for at home their entire life? What have you done to plan for this? Do you or your partner have a cut-off age for giving them the boot to the streets? For example, I was so distraught over the suck my dick conversations (see Chapter 13, Meal Times at Our House) in our home that I began deciding in the back of my mind — 18, that's it! They are OUT! OUT! OUT! Time may change my point of view; the point is...to have the conversation. Learn and know each other's limits to giving your children room and board. This is worth talking about more than once. Along with this conversation comes the conversation about financial support as stated above.

Wedding Funds — Oh yes, I came from the traditional model, as you already know. Discuss wedding plans, if you have any. What do you plan for each other (if you are not already married) and for your kids? Big, small, near home, abroad, city hall or not at all...How much is a wedding worth? What is more important a wedding, a honeymoon, or something else? How much do you plan to help your children financially when it is their turn for this event? Later on how much do you plan to spend for anniversaries each year? How about the big anniversaries, 10, 25, and 50, yours and those of your children?

Let's ask questions about vacations with children (you may also want to view the Travel section of this chapter). Vacations are expensive when multiplied by you, your partner, and the number of kids you have. To mitigate costs, vacations can take the form of backyard adventures in tents! Most importantly, have fun and talk about all the DREAM trips you plan to take! You will not be able to take a dream trip that you never take the time to imagine and plan!

Vacations come in many forms. Do you drive to your destination, take a train, a boat, or a plane? Do you stay in hotels, hostels, tents, yurts, tree houses, other peoples' homes or resorts? Do you go to hot climates or cooler climates? Do you go to other countries or explore on your own? Are the trips active or more sedentary? Do you go to historical sites or hysterical places, like the largest non-living dinosaur on Route 66?

**STOP: *Time to take some notes!***

Since we are in the section about children, talk about what ages your kids will be on these trips: early in life, infant, toddler, child, high school, college, and even when they leave the home. Next up — religion and stuff like that.

## Spiritual/Religion/Philosophy

My spiritual, religious, and philosophical practice all revolve around three things: taking personal responsibility, an attitude of gratitude, and generosity of spirit. How I get from where I am daily to where I'd like to be is my personal quest for being the best me. I believe in a higher power. I pray or meditate on a regular basis. I believe that we are not given challenges that are too big for us, but sometimes we need to dig deeper than we ever thought possible to come into our own awareness.

Take Action. What does having a spiritual life mean to you? Is organized religion important, if so why? What organized religion(s) are you committed to? What is your philosophy on life? Do you practice alone, or do you expect your partner to be included in this part of your life?

## Conscious Curiosity | 163

> *Every question is a hypothetical question for everyone but the person who asks it.* — Dan Savage

How much time do you devote to spiritual practices? Every day, once a week, once a month or hardly ever, get specific. For example, last year I checked myself into a monastery for four days. I had some deep thinking to do around family issues and events that involved my children. Do your spiritual practices include 100% solitude? Do you give yourself permission to take the time you need to grow spiritually?

### STOP: Time to take some notes!

Often when we are a part of organized religious or spiritual practices money becomes a factor. How do you feel about giving donations, cash, and volunteer hours? Commitment and expectation of the tithing of these resources can vary from person to person and from organization to organization. What do you expect you will contribute, if anything?

While I was raising my children and bringing them through their first Holy Communion in the Catholic Church I spent a great deal many more hours volunteering at the Catholic Church than I have at any other time in my life. I treasure those hours. I treasure all that I was able to learn through being a Sunday school teacher, a lectern, and a volunteer at the various Holiday Bazaars. One day I may go back to service in the Catholic Church, but for now developing my own spiritual life on my own terms is far more gratifying.

Take Action. Do you do stuff because you feel like you are supposed to do things a certain way or do you practice stuff because there is a well worn path of "that's the way I have always done it." What if your spiritual and philosophical life path became about what you needed to do to grow and develop your own inner peace and beauty? What if doing so created shifts in your relationship with your partner? Talk about this and other possibilities of aligning your heart with your religious practices.

Organized events are a large part of many spiritual, religious, and philosophical practices. What organized events are important to you? How many do you plan to attend each year, week or month? Are you or your partner in a leadership role contributing to these events? If you are a leader, how long do you plan on doing this sort of work? Do you earn money or are you working 100% in a volunteer capacity?

### STOP: Time to take some notes!

Worth asking again, do you participate in spiritual and religious practices together as a couple or apart? What does being religious mean to each of you? What does being a spiritual person mean to each of you? You may be wildly surprised with each others responses, if so what can you learn from one another? Are your philosophies on life similar or wildly different? What can you learn from one another?

You may have noticed that I separated religion, spirituality, and philosophy as separate ideas. You may find that you want to talk about these words and their meanings — how the differ and what is the connection between them.

If you feel you are not religious or spiritual in any way, why? Do you have a philosophy on life? What can you share? What do you hold dear? What makes no sense at all to you and what changes do you wish to see in the world? What changes do you feel you will be a part of? Honor each other and gain insight to our vast universe through each other's viewpoints.

There is an entire other realm of personal philosophies and practices that needs some paper time here. For lack of better terminology, I will use the Barnes and Noble Book Store categorization of: New Age. Metaphysical and pagan practices are and should also be included in this section. There are very likely other names, terms, and practices that I may or may not be familiar with, list them and talk about them with your partner.

These practices do deserve talk time and similar questioning as the conversations I outlined above in this section. If you use Tarot Cards, Spirit Wisdom, Energy Healing, Animal Cards, Astrology, Numerology, Palm Reading, Handwriting Analysis, Yoga, and/or any other practices, please take the time to talk to each other about these methods for self-development and enlightenment and share your ideas with one another. I could give more paper time to all these wonderful practices and philosophies. Instead, I will leave the terminology and definitions to you and trust that you will take the time to fully realize the importance of spiritual practices to each of you in your lives and in your relationship.

## Politics and Activism

For some, politics and activism constitutes a huge portion of every day, for others this section will encompass a mere fraction of their time and energy. You will be looking to discuss where you fall on the continuum and considering if any changes are required for better quality of life for your relationship.

My husband and I cancel each other out at the voting booth. One of us is a democrat and the other a republican. Since the American system is a two-party system, we as a couple have very likely not voted any change in to action. Rather ridiculous. However, political discussions are fun and we try really hard to learn from one another.

Take Action. Not only at the voting booth, but in your thoughtful responses to the following questions.

Voting — do you vote? Why or why not?

How much time do you spend on politics and activism activities? Do you wish you could spend more time in these activities?

Do you give money to causes? Do you donate your time? Do you donate supplies or professional services?

What causes are most important to you? Do you plan to spend more or less time in the future dedicated to these causes?

Do you believe in activism across borders, or is working within your own community most important to you?

What kinds of clubs or organizations do you belong to and support in the area of politics and activism?

*STOP: Time to take some notes!*

I clearly could use some education in this area to develop better questions for my readers. This book, as I told you, has been written from what I know and what I spend time on in my own life. Neither politics nor activism has been a huge focus in my life. I have not developed a knowledge base in political savvy or activism as I have with other topics. Please do not take this to mean that politics and activism deserve a smaller portion of your skills in conversation. Instead, make time to fully unravel your thoughts and feelings about these important topics. I am open to being further educated and would welcome feedback in the area of politics and activism, especially since I am admitting to my lack of knowledge on these topics.

For the first time ever, I am wondering if part of my lack of passion for the specific details of the issues faced by contemporary society is due to my lack of knowing "home." I have never really been able to deeply know and feel a part of the communities I have lived in — I have always moved too much and did not invest my time in getting to know all the people, places, and issues in my surroundings. Possibly for fear of once again loosing people dear to me or anticipating the need to once again say goodbye. By staying aloof, I keep myself out of politics and the issues facing my neighbors. However, this is an excuse. I know that activism begins from a desire to make change for humanity, our planet, or political reform. Yet, I choose to mainly let things be as they are...

I cannot put my finger on why I have not involved myself in activities to create change. Looking at my thoughts now, my apathy makes very little sense to me. I deeply admire people who have created change for the betterment of humanity. I find great comfort and inspiration in reading the books, words, and speeches of activists, humanists, and feminists. I feel deep gratitude towards people who make difficult choices to make our planet a better place to live.

I know that I am privileged to live the life that I do. I am grateful to women and men before me who have led the way to enacting change in policies that allows for fuller lives for all of us. I feel very sheltered from the important issues of our time that activists all over the world are taking action on, daily. The crux of my apathy could be that I have led too much of a sheltered life. I therefore have no motivation to create waves of change for humanity, for our planet, or for political reform.

I can get on my soapbox, in the form of words in this book, and make pronouncements or ask questions. But my reality is that I am not prepared to die, go hungry, or give up my sheltered existence for movements that are currently underway in society. This is sad. Also, this happens to be my current truth. I am sure that some people will read this aspect of who I am and say, "yep, I knew she was 100% white bread. What a privileged

SOB." I am not happy to read my own words here. This is a sticky situation.

I will understand those who see me as overly privileged and apathetic. In time, possibly I will find what moves me to action, for now let's suffice it to say, I would like the world to be a kinder and gentler place; and if I can add to this by helping couples to have better communication, then maybe this book is my small contribution to the current ills of society.

My other contribution has been in raising my children to be considerate human beings. My plan was to raise them to be independent, happy, and full contributors to our society. They are now at the age where they are finding their own values and voice to bring to the world. However, my role as a parent will continue, always.

If you are politically active and an activist — thank you for your concern. Others of you my be philanthropists instead of activists.

## Philanthropy

You may think this section is only for rich people. However, philanthropy is not only for the wealthy. However, I want you to skip this section if you are sky-high in debt. Please get your own debt under control. Only after you have taken care of your own financial affairs should you consider adding your money to the pool of societal needs.

My idea of what it meant to be a philanthropist started out when I was 22 years old. I began by donating five dollars a year to my alma mater, Carnegie Mellon University. After each half decade I tried to give more than $5 a year. Imagine my surprise recently when I was contacted as being a distinguished and valued alumnus for all my years of giving! Really, for only $5 a year I was now "distinguished as a "Loyal Scott?" My name was added to the lists of fancy parties and events in my local area? How cool, but that was never my initial purpose.

Five dollars and a commitment to giving every year was all it took. Now I can party with the big leaguers, if I want to! Some years I wondered why I was still giving the donation to a place I had not even visited since 1996. The point is: I started and stayed committed. There are a few other organizations that I have regularly contributed to over the years, and some that I started and stopped contributing to. Philanthropy is something that is 100% in your control. Give what you want, when you want. And clearly no amount is too small!

With social philanthropy funding these days, you can literally give to ANY case that makes your heart beat harder, makes you cry, or brings you joy. Think hard about what you believe in. Do the research to find who is already solving the problem you see or start your own cause.

Take Action. Will you give cash or stock in the name of an organization or cause you believe in? What percentage of your income do you expect you'll give on an annual basis? Would you rather give stuff or time?

*STOP: Time to take some notes!*

To what types of organizations do you feel your contributions should go? Schools, nature, science, art, cancer, women's issues, water, food, other... Make your list, have your partner make a list and then share ideas with each other.

Alright, enough about giving, how about parties!

## Birthdays, Celebrations, and Other Big Events

Birthdays, celebrations, and other big events have to do with commemorating time, people, religious holidays, history, life, death, and other stuff. Personally, I believe that many events are over-celebrated! What I mean is, too much food, too much alcohol and overly excessive purchases. Ok, having said that, my humbug attitude is an opinion, not doctrine.

Now, let's continue. There are also other problematic features of celebratory event planning. The big problems are that of past history, family tensions, and money. Nonetheless birthdays and other big events are a part of life and they are a part of mastermind planning for couples. So let's get to it, shall we?

Take Action. List the events you consider to be BIG. Once you have a list compare it with your partner. What had you forgotten and what had your partner missed? What celebrations can you agree on as being "most important?"

**STOP: Time to take some notes!**

What do you do at these events? Provide plenty of detail. How do you spend your time at these events? How much financial investment is required? Do you travel to attend these types of events? How far are you willing to travel? Do you plan ahead and budget big events such as parents' and sibling milestone anniversaries or birthdays?

Do certain celebrations or events bring up bad past memories for you or your partner? How do you plan to address these issues and honor each other's feelings and emotions?

Another aspect of birthdays, celebrations, and events is gift giving. Do you give gift cards, real gifts, or no gifts? What is the norm in your immediate family?

There are families that celebrate with 40 or more guests every year for the same event at the same home and they do this at all costs…for decades. Some people I have talked to light up and cherish the memories that these ongoing events create, other people start dreading their traditions months ahead of the event. Birthdays, celebrations and other big events deserve careful and considered conversation. This section can also include conversations about traditions for other holidays such as Valentine's Day, St Patrick's Day, Cinco de Mayo, and other typical celebratory events.

Parties create messes, so we will jump into a discussion of chores next!

## Chores

Take Action. Let's jump right into this section! Who does the chores in your house? Are you a chore-free household and things keep piling up to the point of being on the reality TV show called Hoarders? Well, why not? There are so many other wonderful tempting things to do to fill life with–so why clean, cook and do errands? Pointless right? Not so fast…

When a home gets filled with too much stuff, dirt, grime and garbage – life can stagnate. There is a reason why Feng Shui has become and is so popular in the Western world. There is a reason why there is a whole industry for the ideas around "clear your clutter, clear your life." There is a reason why the hiring of professional organizers has become a growing industry. I can get political here and list the foibles of our consumerist culture, but that will not support the needs of the mastermind focus needed around "chore time." Family chores can pretty much suck, unless you like to do them.

I hate lots of chores. I hate: toilets, vacuuming, cleaning floors, and grocery stores. I hate it when my boys leave trails. I hate it when stuff does not get put back were it belongs. I hate doing everyone else's dishes. I hate clutter that is not my own clutter. Oh, that's enough ranting!

Back to the topic of chores! Whose responsibility are all of the household chores? What level of cleanliness can each of you live with?

- Laundry, folding and putting away
- Dishes
- Groceries
- Food Prep
- Dry Cleaning/Ironing
- Vacuuming
- Bathrooms
- Bed making
- Kitchen cleaning: including the refrigerator, drawers used most often (food bunnies), and appliances both big and small
- Dusting
- Changing the bed sheets
- Changing the toilet paper rolls
- Changing diapers
- Mending ripped clothing
- Polishing shoes
- Windows and window coverings
- Floors — don't you sometimes wish they were all cement?
- Spider webs in unusual places
- Outdoor debris and overgrowth
- Furniture, for example, couch crumbs, water stains and shit like that
- Sporting equipment maintenance and storage
- Holiday preparation and storage

Gardening and yard work
  Garbage
  Donation of goods trips
  Drug store/prescription runs
  Specialty item errands
  Cleaning cars and other vehicles
  Other — and we KNOW there is a lot of other! List them in your notes, or draw them!

Do you divide the work evenly? Do you constantly avoid some of the work? Do you hire out some of the work? How would chores be handled in a perfect world for you and your partner? What step(s) can you take to get to the perfect scenario?

*STOP: Time to take some notes!*

Do you need to give up some extracurricular activities to make more time for chores? Yes, because what is done or gets left undone in the chores realm could adversely affect the enjoyment of your life on so many other levels! Have the hard conversation around this.

*Do you want to move through a rocky patch in your relationship? Choose long-term growth and integrity; be sure to reject immediate gratification. Simple, done.*

For me, the hard conversation is how much I would *love* to have a cleaning person come once every single week. I love a clean house. I hate doing the work. I have no problems whatsoever in getting the house cleaning-lady-ready so that I can have a super tidy house one evening a week. I am even happy to work alongside anyone else cleaning, but I hate the job of cleaning alone! A weekly cleaning person would be my dream. Only intermittently have I made it happen... hum, maybe time to re-look at this topic! In reality however, I do see a cleaning service as a luxury purchase.

***STOP:** Time to take some notes!*

Your turn. Open up your Pandora's box of chores and divvy up the work. Dig up the crap and make one very necessary step in the right direction for both of you, you can always come back to this section. Make ONE change. The work will always be here. Laundry, cleaning, weeding, and most household chores are NEVER EVER FINISHED! I can never have that feeling of accomplishment like I can with an art project, writing a blog article, or some other type of work that has and end product. As soon as I put away the last of the dishes, I get thirsty and the cycle repeats like a record at the end scratching away at your eardrums, tedious and horrible. Hopefully you know the record player sound I am referring to?

Ok Moving on! Family care is next.

## Family Care and Elder Care

I cannot speak knowingly on the topic of family care and elder care. I have not had to take care of an elder or ill family member, at least not yet, not for any long-term care. However, I have friends that have children and family members that need fulltime care for life. One thing that was and is apparent to me in this situation is that these families accepted outside help on a regular basis. I could never know how difficult it must be to find and plan for long-term care. I admire my friends and the courage they find to do the right thing for their particular family situation. My friends in this scenario have taken different paths to caring for their loved ones while simultaneously caring for themselves. I know that faith, and having a higher power to call on, can be helpful in these situations.

I have had sick children and my husband has become ill once in a while, but I have not had to deal with chronic and on-going health conditions that require long-term care. I can only speak from what I know. What has worked for me in my short-term care providing. I know one thing for sure: I do my best to show up! When my grandfather died, I showed up to help clean some stuff out and to pay respects. When my grandmother was hospitalized, I showed up and stood in line for several hours to get her the meds she needed for her discharge. In this situation, my help allowed my aunt to stay by her side. When my grandmother died, I showed up with my Mom's favorite treat and a willingness to do whatever needed to be done to clear her space. I also gave lots of hugs and lent open ears.

When my mother-in-law was hospitalized for several days I showed up, brought her a few toiletries and I brushed her hair. If I lived closer, and did not have a family of my own to care for, I might have been able to do more. When my other grandfather began to loose circulation in his legs I went to visit him, a long plane ride away. I went with him in the hospital to the compression tank. I sat with him and we talked during his treatment. My other grandmother had Alzheimer's and I was not able to show up because she was a double plane ride away and I was busy with two little boys under age five, but I would have if I could have.

I have never had to be a full- or part-time caretaker – other than my own two children. I have only landed in places where a little help seemed to make a big difference. Still, conversations about "the-what-ifs" has a place in every committed relationship.

We regularly ask our parents what they feel their wishes are for possible elder care, hospitalization or assisted living. Only they can make the decision about what is best for them. Only we can make the decision on what is best for each of us and for our relationship.

I would imagine that the best possible course of action if and when you are in a situation where elder care and family care is necessary is to get help. Emotional help, physical help, medical practices help, and other family members help, and yes, financial help whenever possible.

*STOP: Time to take some notes!*

Take Action. If you are like us, where we really have not had to have these conversations at least play devil's advocate and ask each other the what ifs... Every single response is likely to change and be different in the real situation, but at least you will have opened up and begun the conversation. What if...ask it.

A dear friend of mine has literally no extended family. For her, friends are a life-blood to a life well lived, to connection, and support. Let's look into how friends add to your life.

## Friends

Oh divine spirit, help me write this section! How do you find and keep friends? How do you find couples that can become friends? How do you maintain friendships? For me, this section of life has been a moving target. Literally. Remember back when I told you I have lived in 38 addresses? The truth is — moving frequently makes it much harder to develop close friendships or at least close friends that live a stones throw away!

I have absolutely no solid advice on how to build and increase friendships in life! And yet, I do have dear friends that have been in my life for 20 to 30 years! Except, they do not live nearby. I keep these friendships alive by building travel into my yearly plans.

Still, if you want more, or better, or closer friendships, you'll need to work on making this happen. If you want to decrease the time spent away from your partner, due to too many friends taking too much of your time, you'll need to take a look at what friendships are a barrier between the life you want and the one you have with your partner. Let's look at some possible scenarios.

The friends I maintain are people I met doing something I love to do, for example, while volunteering, working out, going to school, or making art. I know other people meet friends through following sport teams or regularly visiting religious institutions. Couples with kids tend to meet other families with children, through their children's pursuits. Many people maintain friendships that are also work relationships. Of course, there are hundreds of other ways to build friendships and extended relationships into your lives together.

Take Action. What ways have worked for you to find and keep the friends you cherish? If you are looking to build more friendships into your life, what more can you do to increase the chances of building deeper connections with people outside your current realm? If you are looking to feel less pulled into too many circles of friends, what relationships are giving you the most angst? What relationships are costing you in terms of emotional and social health? When you say yes, to events, parties, and outings are you saying yes because you want to or because you are feeling the need to keep face and continue to show up "because you always have"? Do you do regular check-ins to asses if certain events fill your life or drain your energy?

How many friendships do you have personally? How many do you have as a couple? Are there too many relationships to nurture, enough, or not enough? Is it time to let go of the relationships that are not bringing complete joy and health to you and your committed relationship? If so, what's the plan for doing this? What big and small shifts need to happen to make change real?

How do you spend time with your friends? How do you wish you could spend time? How did you meet the top three people you spend time with? How can you build what you want into you life? What one step could you take to get closer to what you want with nurturing friendships?

What ages are your friends? Does it matter if they are older or younger? Is there a pattern of older or younger friendships? What do friendships with people of different ages bring to your life? What would you give up if all your friends were the same age?

Are your partner's friends different from what you would pick? In what ways are the friendships different? Are the differences beneficial? How so? Is different the wrong word? What is it that you do not like about your partner's friends? Please remember to only be honest, open, and kind when talking about this topic. Your partner's friends are of utmost importance to their identity, by ripping on your partner's friends, you could be poking meanly at your partner's identity. Don't do that. Tread carefully on this subject, but certainly do not sidestep it! There can be much growth through unearthing the why of each other's friendships. Why are certain friendships deeply important?

What is the average income level of the friends you most often spend time with? Is the income level higher or lower than your current income level? (I realize most of this is educated guesswork, but it bears recognizing). Some people would say that the question of income level and financial stability or instability is irrelevant in friendships. That may be true. Or it may not. If you are attempting to strengthen your relationship to money, it may not be in your best interest to hang out with people who freely spend huge wads of cash, especially if you do not have that kind of money to freely spend. Alternately, continuing to spend time with friends that cannot afford to do some of the things you wish to do is a way of limiting the dreams you may have for your life.

Spending time with people who have a lot of money (or at least a lot more than you have) that they put to good use in foundations, donations, and helping people to build community or solve some of the world's biggest problems may help you to unleash wonderful ideas for your life that you may never have seen as possible. Who could you meet that would bring your understanding of cash flow and philanthropy to a level above your own? Does it interest you to pursue this course of action? What step could you take to level-up your friends? What if leveling-up meant finding healthier friends, friends with more friends, more educated friends, or something else?

Think about money and all the baggage that comes with it, beginning in school. School age seems to be the approximate age that children begin to internalize the difference of the haves and have-nots. High school is the time when circles of friends form and sometimes these friendships are based on perceived income levels. Do you hold yourself back from certain types of people based on old mental models of what people where like in high school? What are those types? Name them, talk about them. How do these friendships, or lack of past friendships still travel with you today into your current relationships? What would you like to change? What would you like more of?

Do you travel with friends? Why or why not? Would you like to travel with friends, but you never have? What can you do to put plans for travel in place?

Do you have a budget for friends? You know, birthday gifts, parties, travel, and events together? Maybe, for you, money and friends should not be in the same sentence?

What are your thoughts on lending money to friends? Do you do it or not? Why? If you do what is the highest limit? This is serious. I would gladly lend 5 to 40 dollars knowing that I could care less if I ever see that cash again. But a thousand, I have never been asked, and I don't think I would. What are your cash sharing and lending limits and for what reasons?

There is no easy transition from friends to clothing, so I will say it like it is: in the next section we will be tuning into thoughts and ideas around clothing.

## Clothing

Why do you think I put clothing in as a relationship conversation starter and mastermind-planning topic? Because, large shoe collections cost a ton of moola! LOL, while that is certainly true, there is more to it than that. Clothing also talks about image. Remember the section on: What kind of couple do you want to be? Clothing is a component of how you will be perceived by others.

The clothing we wear is like putting on a daily costume to play a role in our relationships and in our communities. That is a big statement. Think it isn't true? Consider a wardrobe 180°. What would such a statement make to your daily peeps? For example, start wearing....ok I cannot do it, I cannot write a particular way of dressing down and then pretend to not have an opinion about it! I am sure you know what I am saying here, what you wear does say something about who you are, even if you are not consciously attempting to say anything. Clothing does this because of cultural norms.

Clothing is important for so many reasons: Perceived sexiness of certain outfits, practicality, comfort, sporty, bad taste, over done, and so much more. Clothing is also an expense. Since creating a Mastermind plan is also about looking at cash flow, clothing had to be a part of the equation of building your best relationship foundation.

Take Action. What is the clothing budget? Seriously, get honest here. Let's not act like our US government...how about we stick to our budgets! Better yet, spend less than you did last month or last year on clothes. Wear your clothes until they really need to be replaced due to wear, not style.

*STOP: Time to take some notes!*

What kind of clothes do you plan to continue to wear? What would your partner like you to give up? Are you willing to change what you wear to make your partner happy? How much are you willing to change? If you are not willing to change your image for others, why not? Be clear, be honest, and most of all be loving.

What type of stores do you frequent? Why does this matter? Because, a good thrift store can have equally good clothing as Neiman Marcus, Kate Spade, Brooks Brothers, Supreme, Lululemon, or RVCA – the only difference being a season or two out of date. The other difference is that at one store the stuff is brand new and at the thrift store the clothing might have been worn. One store takes a wad of cash, the other not as much.

Do you buy clothing specific to sports and activities? Running, hiking, climbing, and biking all have different shoe needs. Yoga is different from karate. Surfing has different needs from skiing. How many sports you participate in can affect how big your sport-specific clothing needs are. Add fly-fishing, camping, horseback riding, and hunting and we have a whole new set of needs. Then add Broadway shows, galas, and art events and we are really increasing the closet size! What is most important? What can be left out?

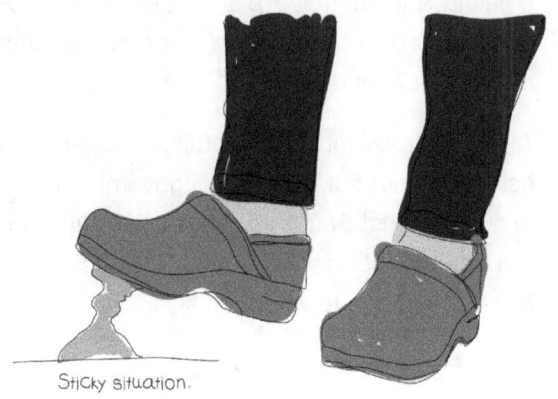

Sticky situation.

One last sticky issue: Shoes. I like to always have at least two pair of running shoes in my closet at all times; one pair that is new and super cushy and one pair that if they were to get sand in them at the beach, I would still be ok. For years, I was teased in our family for buying too many pairs of running shoes each year. Very stupid thing to get teased about! I think my husband has too many USC emblazoned clothing pieces! But I tolerate it, because seriously, there are bigger issues to concern myself with. What clothing sticky issue is there in your life? I know there is one, lay it out on the table, and have the conversation. Be open, be trusting, and be prepared to learn a little more about each other. I did, and I do not get teased any more, thank goodness!

Speaking of shoes, does one of your hobbies require special shoes?

## Hobbies

When is a hobby a hobby, and when is it a business? When is the hobby a wonderful joint or solo pursuit, and when is a hobby an excuse to spend money and avoid the relationship? Yes, I said that! I've seen this tragedy.

Hobbies are an excellent way to learn new skills, blast stress, meet new friends, and challenge your self. No matter your age or skill level you can always find a group to join and learn a new thing or two through hobbies. Hobbies can turn into career changes too!

Take Action. How many hobbies do you partake in, alone or as a couple? Do you want a joint hobby? Does your partner want to try something new with you? What are you willing to try together?

*STOP: Time to take some notes!*

Hobbies can take up large chunks of time. How often do you plan on pursuing your hobby? Will your pursuits take time every day, once a week, once a year, or less?

How much do you anticipate spending on your hobby each year? Are there travel costs related to your hobby? Are there employee or contractor wages to be played to finance your hobby? If you think this question is off the mark, consider car collectors or boat owners. Also consider quilters that have portions of their projects contracted out, and so on…

Make a list of ten hobbies you would love to try in your lifetime. Compare your list to your partners list. Do you have any common interests? If not, do you have interests that spawned new possible ideas for fun things to try together? Hobbies add fun to life. Be bold and courageous and list things here that you would never do in your serious life or in your business life. Do you want to build a canoe out of Legos? How about a yard sculpture out of ping-pong balls? Think of crazy fun stuff that comes up for you in daydreams. Is there a hobby hidden there?

Some people turn their love of pets into a hobby or a business. Let's get personal about pets.

## Pets and Animals

I am a dog lover. I love to live and work with a dog by my side and in my life. My husband does not relish nor does he understand the joys of dog ownership. He sees dogs as, "yet another expense" and "another thing to worry about." However, my dog is by my side as I write this paragraph. Actually, she is jumping up and racing to the door right at this moment because the FedEx driver is dropping off a package. I could not (ok, I choose not) live without a pup. Sure, this is selfish of me, especially in light of my husband's complete and utter distaste for having a household pet. But, there you have it, I have a dog, her name is Luna Blue, she is by my side all of the time. Kenzie, before her, was in the same spot and so was Scout, before Kenzie.

I live much of my time inside my head and imagination. I spend huge amounts of time alone. Luna forces me to take walks and go outside. I relish the times we spend outside together they, and she, make me a happier person. She forces me to pay attention to the time of day. She forces me to stop, listen, touch, care, and breathe and laugh. This joy I feel is constantly kept in check during the times when Luna jumps on my husbands lap and tries to engage him and he says, "off." My joy is also kept in check every time my husband asks me, "how much did that cost?" when referring to her vet bill or a recent boarding stay or a new collar, toy, or leash.

I knew this would be our truth when I rescued her. Childish as I am, I harbored hopes of change, like oh, this time he will fall in love with the dog...I was wrong. She is mine and we live together...with him.

This is so bloody painful to write! Fuck!

Anyway, let's get on with things, shall we? Once in a while you will make choices that your partner does not care for.

Take Action. Ask each other all sorts of questions about pet ownership — large and small — and for your sake, I pray your situation is easier than mine.

*STOP: Time to take some notes!*

Side note: It is a new month. Husband and Luna are learning to be a grand part of each others life...one day at a time they are finding how to be around each other...he even takes her out on short walks — or is it her taking him?

She greets him every night when she hears the garage door open and close, I am not sure how much he likes her enthusiastic jumpy greeting, but there you have it. She says hi each night, then it's my turn to say hi.

Little Luna volunteers her love again and again and again, expecting nothing in return. Do you give of your time expecting nothing in return?

## Volunteer

Why do I put volunteer in the Mastermind section? The first reason is because I believe in offering volunteer hours to strengthen the community I live in or the world at large, and also volunteering can be a way to learn new skills or offer personal unique skills to others. The second reason is because volunteering in any small capacity every week, month, or year can add joy and richness to life. Remember I said that I see a more beautiful and peaceful world in my imagination? Volunteering my time helps me to know that I am adding to the picture in my mind for our planet. In many ways volunteering has been my way of being involved in political stuff – I donate my time, talent, and money in places I feel our government is lacking in services to society.

Volunteering can come in the form of volunteer board positions, donations of goods and services, and publicly fundraising. There are charity events and church bazaars and many other ways of being in service either in your immediate community or around the world. Pick something you believe in, find out what you have to offer, and then volunteer.

Take Action. Are you a regular volunteer or are you someone who has never volunteered? If you have, what do you do? If you haven't, what do you think you'd like to offer? If you never want to volunteer, feel free to skip this section *after* you discuss with your partner why volunteering is or is not important to you and why volunteering is or is not important to your partner.

*STOP: Time to take some notes!*

Certain issues are important to address when considering volunteer hours. Do not volunteer if you barely have enough time and money to keep your own roof over your head and food on the table, but be honest with yourself about this. Do you spend huge amounts of time on on-line games, watching TV, or surfing the net? If so, could volunteering and learning a new skill possibly bring you much more satisfaction over the course of a lifetime. Many skills built in volunteer work can transfer to your job. Even when my husband and I utilized the United States WIC (Women Infant and Children) program, I still found a few hours a month to volunteer, that's how important giving and being a part of my community has always been to me. But that's me and you are you. What would work for you?

Would you rather volunteer at a leadership level and hold an office position? What industry or organization are you most fond of? What skills can you offer? My husband has served on numerous Homeowners Association boards, each time that they find out that he's a "finance guy" they want him to work on the budget for the HOA board. He usually says yes for a year or at most two years at a time. He'll take a break and wait to be asked again. Over the years I have watched him wisely keeping his limits and leaving room for other pursuits.

Volunteer jobs are real jobs! You need to show up and do the work. You will build relationships and you will be counted on to make a difference, but you will not get paid and sometimes you will not get thanked. You must draw your boundaries; you must be honest with the organization that is counting on you. I say all of this because volunteering is about giving your full time and attention to the organization that you have decided to align yourself with, but sometimes the relationship goes sour. What is the "line in the sand for you?" What would have you saying, "I'm done with this," and move on. Write down your thoughts, commit to the job that sounds fun and challenging and do the work. But remember to always honor your "line in the sand," because other organizations could use your time and talent. Don't get too burnt out, find what works for you and carry on.

There is also another line in the sand that needs to be addressed. At what point does the volunteer work take away from your relationship? If it does, how long will you work this way? How long can your partner watch you over-commit? I have seen relationships totter on thin ice and some even eventually fail due to the partner over-committing to his or her volunteer pursuits (along with other reasons to be sure). Don't let this happen to you!

Sometimes being a volunteer means more than your time and talent. Sometimes you also need to serve up some cash. Yes, there are volunteer jobs where you pay to work. I know it sounds counterintuitive, but that's the way things are. Decide before you sign up what you can afford, and stick to your budget. What is your amount? Is there a per year amount, or per month? Write it down. Review the number with your partner. What does he or she think about your need to pay to work as a volunteer? This is a real conversation starter!

Volunteering does not only take your cash, talents, and skills it also takes your time.

## Time

There are a million ways to measure time, but in the end we all have the same number of hours per day. It is completely up to us how we decide to use our time. I think it is nearly impossible to talk about time and not also address the topic of earning a living, or work.

For most people, jobs are an everyday reality and the expectation is to show up for a set number of hours, often more than 45 per week. The company then pays you for your time. The time left over is used for all other life pursuits. There are other ways to look at time, but let's stick with the time-job picture here for a moment.

Take Action. I have introduced time in hours equaling a return of money. What if you only wanted to work 20 hours per week for your current or a higher yearly gross? How can you reach your target? What job would you do that gets paid the correct amount per hour to reach your target? Many entrepreneurs these days set themselves up for passive income revenue streams. If you don't know what that is, take the time to learn about the many varied ways of earning a living and decide if there is something new that you can build into your life and change how your time is allocated.

*STOP: Time to take some notes!*

I value my time in terms of flexibility. If I want to work out in the middle of the day, eat dinner at 4PM, and visit a child at school in the middle of the week, I can. I have built my life into having the ability for this flexibility. I earn an income through being a landlord, which is a form of hands on passive income stream. I also earn money selling my art, teaching art classes and hopefully from selling copies of this book.

The reality is however, that time is unfairly divided in our home. My husband works gobs and gobs and gobs of hours every day, every week, every month and from year to year. In order for me to maintain my flexibility and service our family, we have a lopsided system. He works for others. I work for us. Neither of us has been able to uncover a way to change the problematic division of time. I suppose this could be because on some level our system is working for us.

Take Action. How do you value your time? By how much you make per hour? By the flexibility you have or don't have? By how much time you have to do sports and other activities? By how much time you have to spend with family and friends? Hobbies? Other?

*STOP: Time to take some notes!*

We all have 24 hours in a day. How do you chop up your day? How do you make it flow? How do you spend your time? How do you wish you could spend your time? What steps can you take to get there?

Do you need time each day, month or year for individual alone time? How much? How frequently?

How much time would you ideally like to spend together with your partner? Is one weekend a month enough? Every weekend? How many hours per day? If you and your partner have different ideas about "together time" how do you collaborate to find the best amount of time so that you both feel honored in your needs for time together?

This concludes the list of topics on our treasure hunt for creating a life well lived together. Keep in mind that the best mastermind plans are created with help — mastermind mentors.

## Mastermind Mentors

All great Mastermind programs include finding mentors along the way to guide you through and encourage you through tough times, blocks, and big ideas. Find couples that inspire you. Ask them to dinner and ask questions. Let them know how much you value their expert advice. Most people are thrilled to talk about the stuff that is going well in their life. Give them that joy. Find mentors when you need them. Parents can be mentors, next-door neighbors, friends, work acquaintances, couples younger than you, and older. Find mentors related to areas that you feel you could use an extra boost of help. Make sure to say yes to others and lend them an ear when they ask you for a favor.

## Robbing A Bank

When I first began writing and trying the work the Mastermind chapter I honestly thought that two people could go through these exercises and literally create a plan of action for their life together as a couple. Not, possible. Creating life plans that you desire to accomplish are far more risky and way more involved than robbing a bank!

I wish I could give you a story of success here to inspire you to take action and follow through on all the wonderful ideas that you uncovered while studying and doing the work in this chapter. However, creating change takes time — lots of it! I have experienced incremental changes with my husband as a result of this book. We are having more in-depth and idea focused conversations than we have since we were first married. Also, the tips, hints and questions as presented in Conscious Curiosity has led to more time spent together in teeny tiny ways each day for us. We are finding more joy. We make each other laugh more. We push back and forth more — asking each other to be a bigger better self. We have not created a 180° revolution, but you never know...life has a way of presenting opportunities when the time is right.

The next chapter is about following through on capturing the financial issues that you uncovered while doing the work in the Mastermind chapter. Hopefully, you jotted down current numbers, future idea numbers and stuff in your budget you want to, easily can, or will rid yourself of as you push toward dreams. Off you go, the chapter for measuring cash is up next!

# Chapter 7 —
# Fill In the Numbers

> *The biggest mistake that many people make is not in expecting too much from their relationships, but in desiring too little.* — Bloomwork

## Cash

Um, yea, I told you based on my mother's wisdom that I would address communication, collaboration and cash. Well, now we are at the cash chapter. This is the chapter that I am sure more people will ignore than any other. Who wants to talk about money? Money issues are often blamed for discord between people — especially those in close relationships. Money is poopy, and we all spend so much of our lives trying to make more of it!

Time to change attitudes here.

Money is only sexy when you feel like you have enough of it — or at least that is what we tell ourselves right? I bet you'd be hard-pressed to find someone, anyone who feels like they have enough money. Let's take it up a notch — plenty of money. How about it, can you find friends that have (and admit to having) an *abundant* amount of cash? Do those people even exist? A wad of cash versus tightening the belt, that's part of what we will look at in this chapter.

Listen, YES that person exists! That person could be YOU! How? By learning to only spend money on stuff, things, adventures, education, and activities that bring you a gigantic amount of joy and a feeling of abundance. I have an example for you. Can spending money on 2-ply toilet paper make me feel wildly abundant? Why, yes it can!

Tighten your spending.

My parents have plenty of money. I love what they have taught me about using cash to pay for almost everything. Yes, cash, that old fashioned stuff. Using cash means fewer bills to pay at the end of the month! I love them for teaching me the value of operating with cash. However, with Apple Pay, PayPal, direct bank drafts and other forms of electronic payments from our smart phones, cash may soon find itself extinct. I hope not, but I think it is inevitable.

Still, let's talk about the feeling of abundance.

Who regularly honors the feeling of abundance? Let me share a TMI (too much information) story. My parents use single-ply toilet paper (TP) to wipe! Seriously?!? Who does that? Because of their preferred TP usage and example of how to cut corners financially, I feel hugely abundant when I buy 2-ply toilet paper.

I really do! I could choose single ply, like they do. After all I grew up that way and I would save money, especially over the course of a lifetime. Certainly they have! How much? Who knows, you do the math, that's not my strength, or ask my parents, maybe they know. But, naw, for this one utterly important product I am happy with my daily reminder of abundance! I love the feel of softness and absorbency of my 2-ply TP. Toilet paper is one area where I can feel oh so much joy about my (cash) flow!

And for those of you still thinking about the math. The average cost of toilet paper for one person per year is $52. The cost would be less for single ply and more for 2-ply. That's a few thousand dollars over a lifetime. Possibly saving a few thousand dollars would make you feel more abundance in your life? That's for you to decide.

How then, do we cut corners in my house? We eat-in. I cook, often from scratch. We order a small size or even kids size for treats like coffee out or ice cream. A Starbucks or ice cream date often feels like a "treat" because we go out so rarely as a couple. We pay the whole entire VISA bill every month. We say *No* to our kids, often. They are very familiar with second hand shops and the Goodwill. We rarely drink alcohol and we don't smoke. We put money into our IRA and 401k accounts. We "brown bag" our lunch. We use heat and air conditioning sparingly. We have taken many "stay-cations" as a family (taking time off from home base). My husband irons his own shirts for work every week! Ugh, writing all our real honest to goodness money saving methods here feels like I am announcing to the world: We are dull and boring! But if that's what it takes to feel abundant when I buy my 2-ply, then so be it, that's what it takes.

What would it take for you to feel abundant?

Take Action. Use the information you gathered in the Mastermind chapter to create a reliable budget. Go back over each section and think numbers. Highlight the numbers, circle them, or write numbers in bright red ink. These numbers should indicate what you currently spend — Cash Use. What you would like to spend on stuff will come as a later exercise. The list will be huge and unwieldy, I know. What do you really spend your money on? You won't know, until you track.

*STOP: Time to take some notes!*

Use a tracking system or at the very least, find out today's current numbers in spending and saving in every category in your household.

Current Use of Cash (for every section in Mastermind):
Weekly
Monthly
Yearly

Current Use of Cash (for _____):
Weekly
Monthly
Yearly

Current Use of Cash (for _____):
Weekly
Monthly
Yearly

Repeat!

## Chart Your Cash

Here I go again, I once again feel the need to be 100% honest. I have tried to chart and track our spending, but life is full of other wonderful things I like to do (like draw and paint, spend time with family and outdoors, read books, and write books). Don't get me wrong, I do track spending, but not as tight as I could. I do not track our income to the penny. I used to track our cash to the penny when we first got married, but not anymore.

I do manage to look at our budget in detail once a year. I do projections quarterly and determine if we are where we need to be to make ends meet and to do the activities we have planned as well as having enough money for any larger expected or unexpected expenses. Twice a month (sometimes more) I pay our bills. Every week at least once, usually more, I look at our accounts on-line to see if what I know we have spent actually shows up correctly on the accounts. In the Mastermind chapter hopefully you talked about who does this work in your relationship. This work is important work; do not ignore tracking your dollars and balance to the penny if you wish!

Take Action. In this section I would like to suggest that together you create a budget. Such an ugly word, yet, such a necessary activity. Businesses do the work of creating and following a budget to stay in business. You should too, to keep your relationship sustainable, happy, joyful, and full of abundance. You can use an excel spreadsheet, you can use pencil and paper, or you can use an on-line resource like Mint.com or any similar on-line application to create and follow a budget. How you track *your* money is up to you, not tracking your cash is really not an option if you want to keep a steady flow of abundance in your life.

In the previous section you did some collecting of information about what you currently spend. Great. Now, using what you know, create a realistic budget that includes saving cash. If it at all interests you to be a solution to the debt problem in the United States and across the globe use your own budget to work towards living a life without loans.

Take the plunge.

A crazy concept, I know. I am not saying we will all reach that goal. However, I need to let you know that I have had fun trying to live loan free in our family. Let me phrase this concept better, I am having fun each month paying *more* on our loans than the bank tells us we have to. Why is that fun for me? Because I know that the banks will earn less money from us over the long term — that makes me feel abundant even more than my 2-ply TP. Hee hee!

> *STOP: Time to take some notes!*

It is now time for you to take the plunge. What will you do to feel more abundant in your personal financial life? You will need a cheering section, because this tracking, saving, data collection stuff is work. Work worth doing though, don't you think!

Make your own real honest to goodness budget.

## Chart Your Future

Now let's take the idea of tracking cash a step further. For each section in the Mastermind chapter get going on bigger, better, and wilder dreams of abundance. Instead of only knowing what you spend, tracking the cash you spend, and locating places that you can save cash, now you get to project your spending into future dreams, possibilities, plans, and growth.

Take Action. For each section in the Mastermind chapter I want you to pull out all the stops. What would an all out no holds bared amazingly abundant life look like? If you have never dreamed this big and committed the dreams to paper this exercise will feel really hard for you. You may even feel like you should hold back — because who are you to want to own a yacht one day? Who are you to deserve a trip around the world first class? Who are you to want to build yourself a custom home on 5 acres of land? Who are you to want further education and no student loans? What dreams do you have?

Who are you to want to earn so much money that you can give $100,000 away each year or more to your favorite charity? Who are you to want to buy a home for your children? A complete wardrobe and makeover, why not? One month every year at a luxury spa, why not? Have you ever dreamed of a summer home and a winter retreat?

Crap, I am writing this from a white stay-at-home middle aged woman on a chair in my living room — how could I possibly know what would make *you* dance for joy? How could I possibly know what would make *you* feel like you are living a life of abundance? I can't, you need to dream and write and share ideas by yourself and with your partner. Pull out all the stops, create your own dream budget.

Go through every topic in the Mastermind list and dig up *your* dreams. Then, create your perfect dream budget in line with your new goals and values. Keep in mind, abundance might mean not spending money in certain categories as presented. Get real. Get honest.

**STOP: Time to take some notes!**

Use a tracking system and dream about how much you actually would need to reach your wildest abundance in every category in your household.

Future Use of Cash (for every section in Mastermind):
Weekly
Monthly
Yearly

Future Use of Cash (for _____):
Weekly
Monthly
Yearly

Future Use of Cash (for _____):
Weekly
Monthly
Yearly

Repeat!

You could also create a pie chart using the numbers and data you have collected for each life category. Do the pie chart pieces feel like they are the right size when viewed with your goals, dreams, and values in mind? If not, how and what changes can you put into place to make the pie sweeter?

And a bonus problem:

There is an Economic Cost of Burn Out. Said another way, reaching for everything (and buying or doing too much) because you are not clear on your own personal dreams, values, and aspirations can create a recipe for burn out.

Burn out can be described in many ways. Burn out can come from trying to do a little of everything that everyone else seems to be doing. Burn out can come from years of not having your finances in line with your values. Burn out equals *not* feeling your *best* because you gave too much to your job(s) in terms of time, emotion, and energy.

The idea for this bonus section is to give the idea of "burn out" and actual value in cash. Burn out comes from giving too much, doing too much and pushing too hard against obstacles that you think you need to drive through. Burn out is real, and deserves your attention. Burn out robs you of a beautiful life.

Once you have a number value, in cash, for burn out, then put a value on self-care. What it would take for you to *feel* really great. Think of these numbers in terms of a month or a year, even using just one week might work as well. Below is a sample, you'll need to devise your own chart details.

Economic Cost of Burn Out

1. missing work, lost wages or lost income in your business
2. doctors visits, in time, misspent energy, gas
3. the cost of doctors visits, in cash $20-$70 each, plus more for ambulance/hospital/other
4. the cost of ill health years and years from now and even today

5. other hard to define items that make you feel burnt out, but there is a number in cash and it is:
6. loosing your paid time off hours from your job because they do not roll over
7. emotional cost, can you imagine and give this a number
8. what price do you put on waking up each morning to do the work you do not love?

Total Dollar Amount of burn out: How much? (Could this number as high as $10,000 or even more?)

Now, figure out a way to measure the cost of taking really good care of yourself.

Investing in Self Care.

1. leaving work early or on time one day a week (take a bike ride, take a nap, do an errand, or go outside, start to learn something new)
2. eating healthy, and spend time making the food
3. equipment for doing the sport or hobby you love
4. using paid time off, free
5. learning yoga or meditation
6. picking up a hobby you love
7. massage each month or week, $25-$65 or more
8. other self-care needs
9. paying all your bills on time every time, bonus: no extra fees
10. hugging your significant other or children with wild abandon
11. ridding yourself of 100 items that you have not used in a year, do this over and over again every three months and…you may find room for growth in other areas of your life

Total Dollar Amount of self-care: How much? (Is this number less than the cost of burn out? Hint: Often it is, but we are afraid to do the right thing and take care of ourselves.) Here is the formula:

Burn Out − Self Care = Your Healthy Price

You found the number, good for you. Add this number to your weekly, monthly, and annual budget. The idea here is to realize that working harder to make more money is sometimes not the answer to feeling and living better. Seeing the real numbers can shed light for some people on the best course of action.

That's it for the Mastermind chapter; we've covered a lot of territory. In the next chapter we will explore communication again, this time non-verbal communication. What's that you say? Communicating without talking? Turn the page and let's continue to be consciously curious.

# Chapter 8 —
# Non-Verbal Communication

> *I think we live in a time of distraction and disassociation. People seem further and further removed from the reality they live in, constantly leaping between virtual experiences in the palms of their hands. So I think it's crucial to find a way to spend some time in the here and now, the actual reality we inhabit, not filtered through Facebook and Instagram and Netflix and YouTube. I love technology but I worry that if we spend too much time in unfiltered reality, we will lose touch with what matters, we'll care less about the consequences of our actions, we'll become utterly plugged-in and tuned out.*
> — Danny Gregory

## Touch the Ones You Love

I almost forgot to write this chapter! Then I woke up one morning regretting that I had not hugged my husband the night before. Bingo! A new chapter is born.

> *Do you touch the ones you love often enough?*

Sometimes, oftentimes, non-verbal communication is more powerful than words. Often, non-verbal communication is used in negative ways between people in committed relationships.

The thing is, I don't really want to talk about all the negative signs and symbols that we send out on a regular basis — you know, pouting, storming out, crunched foreheads and worse types of non-verbal communication, including violent non-verbal communication. I myself participated in negative non-verbal communication the other night when I did not properly say goodnight to my husband! I want to focus on positive non-verbal communication, not the missed opportunities or the actual really bad stuff like hitting or throwing things.

If you are in a relationship with seriously negative and abusive non-verbal communication, like being hit or having things thrown at you, the best thing to do is to work on an exit strategy. Work on improving your situation every single day. No one deserves abuse! Get professional help, as soon as possible. This goes for verbal abuse as well, do not tolerate it. Get out. Get out as soon as you can. You, my love, can be in a loving and full relationship one day, but not by staying in a negative place. Love yourself and take care of yourself first, you do matter. You matter very much and deserve the best!

Touch is crucial to human survival. Decide for yourself what kind of touch and how often you will use touch to stay connected and communicate your love.

## Hearing Is Not Everything

Non-verbal communication is near and dear to my relationship with my husband. May I tell you why? He is hearing impaired. He was born with his impairment and his family did not learn of his difficulties until he was three years old, when his younger brother was talking more than he could. He cannot hear any high tones or high pitches. Sounds like birds chirping do not exist for him, and many cell phone ring sounds don't register as sound in his ears or brain. He does not hear sounds such as "s," "ch," "ce," or "z" in spoken word. The difference between "j" and "g" and other closely related sounds in words are challenging for him. Knowing when to finish a word with the past tense "ed" or plural form "es" is challenging in both written and spoken language. Daily we live with his disability as a part of our existence together.

As he gets older, he has told me that he feels like his hearing is getting worse, just as so many other aging individuals experience. But he has *less* to loose to begin with, and this makes the future somewhat frightening for him. Amongst his concerns are: will he be able to continue working and will he be able to enjoy talking to those he loves at his current capacity. We do not know. However, there is no use in dwelling on the unknown. We can only have faith that all will be ok, in some fashion or another.

He learned to talk using flashcard pictures and speech therapy. As a child and as an adult, he has been building his natural and learned skills of reading body language and non-verbal cues. He is excellent at reading other people through body language.

He works really hard every single day at work, at home, and in public to listen, and most importantly, to understand. He uses visual clues to fill in the gaps. He hears and sees things in personal interactions that go unnoticed by others. He has a gift. This is a gift that we don't always see as a gift. Some people might think he is slow to understand, and others may get frustrated when he answers a simple question incorrectly. His hearing affects every moment of his daily life.

His hearing affects every waking moment of our life together as well, often, for the best, and many times for the worse. He cannot hear me when I whisper. He cannot hear me if I talk to him while we hug or if I talk while I am crying. I get sick and tired of needing to repeat myself. I get sick and tired of feeling like I am being ignored, when in fact he really did not hear me! I even get sick and tired of being his ears! He will often ask me, "what was that?" when we hear an unusual background sound, in some cases the sound is not really that unusual, but his brain cannot place it because there are missing parts to the sound. We cannot talk in busy crowded restaurants. We don't go to loud concerts. Even talking while in a car or on a bike ride is challenging — he needs to see my face to fully hear me.

There are too many details of living with a man of super power visual acuity and hearing impairment to share them all with you. Let me suffice it to say that, when other people complain that their partner does not listen to them, I cringe. They really have no idea what it is like to not be heard. Of course, there are zillions of other people and couples out there dealing with larger hearing issues and even larger health issues, but I am not here to measure the depths of different peoples pains and health frustrations. I am here to shed light on non-verbal communication as one of the important forms of building communication into your life in a committed relationship.

Hearing is not everything; you need to clue into your inner emotions and those of your partner. You also need to pay attention to visual cues and other non-verbal cues. When I say hearing is not everything I am talking about the hearing we do through our ears. However, there are many other forms of "hearing." We can hear through our heart, through touch, and through remembering to take the time to be in the present moment as much as possible.

## Use All Your Body Parts to Talk

Let's start at the top. Your head has forehead wrinkles, eyebrows, eyes, cheeks, nose, lips, chin, and neck with muscles that can change what you say by how they form facial images. You could be verbally saying, "I love you" while simultaneously saying, "you frustrate me" non-verbally. Try it in the mirror sometime. You will find it really *is* possible to send mixed messages, even to yourself!

Use your face with care when you communicate.

Kisses!

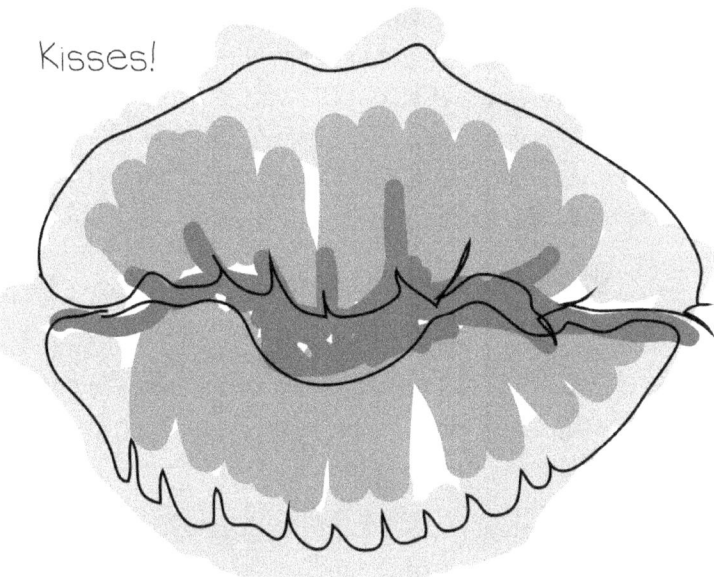

We have posture and body parts that can talk. There are basic cues like crossed arms or legs that say I am here, but I am blocking or protecting myself from some of what you are sharing. However non-verbal communication can have many varied meanings. The same crossed limbs could be saying to the other person that you are mad, don't care, or could even mean the person is feeling cold... because visual cues are complex. There are entire books written on the topic of non-verbal communication, in fact entire bodies of life studies have been devoted to the topic. I am here to ask you to notice your own non-verbal communication.

Use your body with care when you communicate.

> *Did you know that talking is such hard work that moving your hands and arms while you talk can help you to talk more smoothly?*

Take Action. Let's see what can we make work for building better non-verbal communication into your relationship starting today, without years of study. Did you look each other in the eyes and say, "good morning" today? Did you kiss? Did you hug? Did you touch while making breakfast together? Did you offer to help carry extra heavy gear to the car?

*STOP: Time to take some notes!*

Upon seeing each other after the workday did you greet each other with a smile? Did you hug? Did you touch? Did you kiss? Did you help each other in the kitchen preparing an evening meal and cleaning up afterwards?

Yes, these are really basic forms of communication! Yes, the really basic non-verbal communication is super duper important! Why? Because the so-called simple actions lay the groundwork, the foundation for more communication!

Throughout the book I have listed hints and tips of how to approach conversations. I have mentioned stuff like facing each other while you talk. I have shared ideas like sharing the roles of being the scribe. I have suggested setting time to be together without distractions. I have hinted at doing the work together and apart. All of these hints and tips are related to non-verbal communication. Words and listening alone are NOT ENOUGH to feel heard or to be heard. Yes, I mean that!

I know, because I live with a man who relies heavily on what my body is saying to fill in the gaps of what my words are saying. When we first met I was scared shitless about his perceptions of my state of being! He could read me and I did not like it. Yes, having someone that seemed to know how I was feeling before I even knew how I was feeling was terrifying! How the heck could he do that!?!??? How the heck does he know how I feel? ...I remember thinking on numerous occasions. I have since learned more about my own feelings and how I show them on my body.

I now know he was reading my body language! Body language, unless you become an expert in controlling it (actors do this), communicates naturally beyond words. Are you aware of your unspoken language? Dogs are amazing full body communicators, watch them and learn. We have gifts beyond dog, we can write. Writing can serve as another form of non-verbal communication.

## Love Letters

Did you or do you still write love letters to your partner? I find that when things are getting rough or if we have not seen each other for extended conversations for a while due to busy schedules or whatever else life has tossed us; a love letter can go a long why to bridging our communication with one another until the next time we find time for face-to-face conversation. Reawaken the lost art of love letters.

Take Action. Write each other one love note every day for one week. Hide them in special places or mail them. Kiss them or scent them. Invite each other to a secret rendezvous in writing. Love letters can be as small as a post-it note and as long as a good novel; it is up to you to create what feels right.

*STOP: Time to write some love letters!*

Taking the idea of a love letter and expanding on the notion. Do you ever feel like sometimes you can explain things better in writing than you can with spoken words? Why not use this skill with your partner? Put aside a notebook that is reserved for talking through writing. Let's say you have something to say, but you do not know how to say it in words. Use the notebook. Give your partner time to absorb what you have to say and ask them to respond via the notebook.

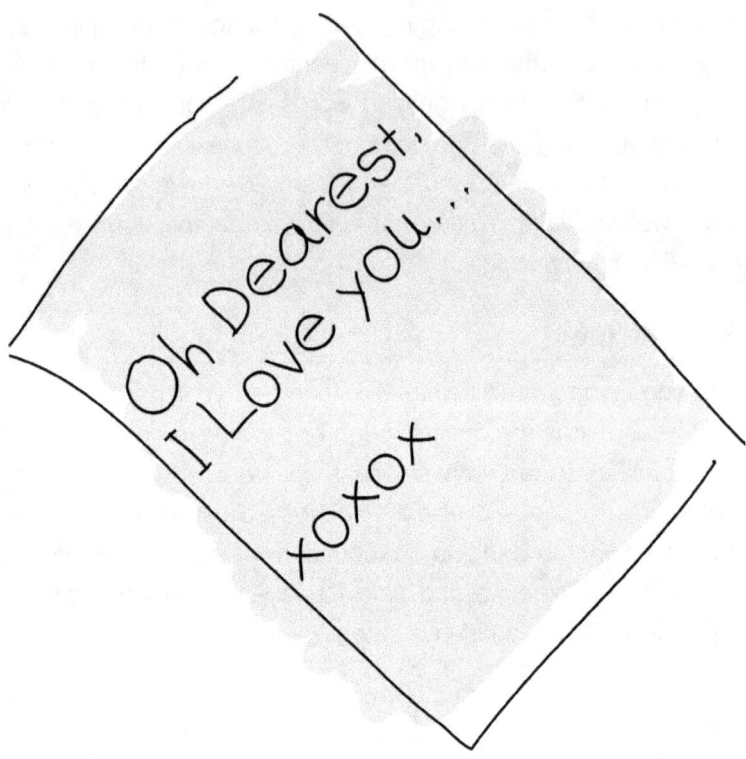

Take Action. Initiate a partner's notebook practice talking to one another through the written word via a notebook. Decide if you respond back within 4 hours or twenty-four hours. Set parameters that work for both of you. Decide what topics are taboo in the written form. For example, maybe you do not want to write: "Let's have sex in the laundry room tonight." But then again, maybe you do. Anyway make The Notebook work for you. Make it safe, and be sure to keep it away from the kids if the topics are for the parent's eyes only.

*STOP: Time to find a suitable notebook and a place to store it.*

We have covered touching, hearing, body language, and writing now it is time to put all of these ideas together and communicate via non-verbal magic.

Our non-verbal cues are doing their magic every single day with one another. Even when both people in the couple are not hearing impaired! Maybe each of you or one of you needs to build skills in the area of non-verbal language — either sending signals or understanding the signals. The first step towards building these skills is to pay attention to them! I believe I have said this before in this book: you can improve skills in areas that you choose to focus on. Pay attention to what you pay attention to, and surely the awareness alone can be a step in the direction of better utilization of non-verbal signals in your communication with your partner.

Take Action. If you find that you need more help in the area of non-verbal communication, then play games together. Make stuff up. Test each other. You can read books together on the subject or watch YouTube videos. There are many good TED Talks on non-verbal communication. Get creative! Spend a whole day not talking, while spending time together. Then talk about what you learned over dinner.

*STOP: Time to take some notes!*

I know that one day I may not be able to have full conversations with my husband, but this could be true for anyone. Hearing aids can only take us so far...and then there could be silence. Intimate connection will be maintained through touch, vision, body language, writing, and our shared history. We are packing our love box full each day through conversation and non-verbal communication. Are you?

We will also potentially have technology to aid us in our continued connection with one another. However, technology can also be a problem even more than financial issues. Read more to find out what I mean.

## The Technology Equation

I would be remiss if I did not address the technology equation in this book. Technology has and will continue to change how people interact in social and personal interactions. I think about this, a lot.

Technology has fast become an additional form of non-verbal communication. I suppose some communication research experts may be arguing that since we do use words to communicate via technology, communicating via technology should be considered verbal communication. Then again, there are likely other researchers that are arguing that communication via technology is non-verbal. I am not in the academic setting at this time, and I have not researched academic journals on this topic. For the purpose of the ideas as presented in Conscious Curiosity, technology creates non-verbal communication scenarios.

Communicating via technology removes two people from face-to-face communication and leaves much room for interpretation of information and error. Words on a screen are not verbal, even short videos are not interactive in the same way that face-to-face communication can be. Skype, and other similar video conferencing sources are excellent and they do appear to be face-to-face interaction, but they still miss context. People being who they are, can tune in and tune out at will with technology as the media for talking.

How we react, behave, and communicate with one another is rapidly changing. Technology and the blend of many cultures is now a reality due to conversations that are being had all over the globe via social media. These conversations are contributing to huge changes in how we all communicate and how we understand. The blend of many voices is good, and I am happy that we are on a path to potential better understanding. However, the other side of the blending or "melting pot" of voices is that more and more often I see people confused about how to talk in person face-to-face. No longer do traditional manners and vocabulary make sense in all situations.

The other day I was working with a plumber and he said, "well, it is easy enough to change, your husband could do...or you, or..." he stumbled on how to continue because he knew he was making assumptions about my living arrangement. I wish communication could have been easier for him, but those days are gone. We are all learning how to be inclusive of each other.

As we head into the holiday season, the stumbling and misfiring of well-wishing exponentially explodes. How do we wish each other well? Happy _____, merry _____, other holiday, or nothing at all? We can't be correct all of the time! Exhaustion from political correctness overtakes us at the end of each day! And is it no wonder? How do we stay true to our core beliefs around religious holidays and simultaneously respect others as well? How do we honor the wonderful differences we all share with the world and simultaneously create meaning?

Technology has created a super highway for a vast amount of communication to take place and allows people to vent and share their opinions. Technology is great at opening up the worlds of other people's voices into our realm. However, making sense of all of the new information takes place in private, at least for now. I believe face-to-face and one-to-one conversations will be the foundation that can contribute to better understanding between all people.

When you know someone on a personal level, you can have better understanding even at a group level. Be it race, sex, age, or other "categorization/label" of humans. I believe, that through learning from one another we *all* can be happier in our relationships!

I am fully aware that this book takes an "in your face" attitude in my style of writing. I toss the darts hard and fast in the hopes that some of the ideas can hit a target. Similar to the internet, there is a seemingly endless array of information and questions. I have been looking for a way for you to find an endless amount of information inside of yourself on what will work for you to increase connection with your significant other in your life.

Similar to the way the internet works when you search for information, this book groups many related ideas. Unlike the internet, the ideas I share are floated out there — most often in the form of questions. Lots of questions, to ask yourself and one another. Drop in on your partner from time to time and ask the questions you dared not ask before.

The internet and social media gives us ways to drop in and eavesdrop unbeknownst to others. Honestly, this practice is really creepy. The strange thing is I have found that, for me, the skill of eavesdropping has spilled into my everyday life, even when I am off the internet. Now I drop in on conversations people not expecting me to be listening to. What I have been doing is searching for ideas. Then the ideas floated their way into this book. I wanted a book that moves ideas about communication forward in full speed-ahead increments.

Now, with my husband, when we utilize some of the content from this book, we ask questions and consciously search for content and we have rich conversations. At other times my husband will fire questions at me instead of answering mine.

Either way, we are dropping in and tuning in — in this way we are not involved in the technology equation, instead we are involved in each other's lives.

I have another habit I utilize in order to drop out of the technology equation. I draw and sketch, often in public. When I am quiet and spending time in public keeping a sketchbook or making a journal entry I am in non-verbal listening and noticing mode. I literally eves drop and listen or watch others conversing. I know, this is unorthodox behavior — maybe not, maybe admitting that I listen in, is the truly unorthodox part. Anyway, I know I am being rude. I get juicy tidbits of nothing or conversation chunks out of context in this this way. The nothing I get from eavesdropping becomes fodder for my thoughts about other people's skills in communication, or lack thereof. Admittedly unfair since I told you I listen out of context. My hope is that by challenging my thinking about what it is that I hear out of context and by attempting to make sense of current trends, I can shed light on skill improvements for couples and for you.

Take action. Stop and think about some of your habits around the use of technology and social media. Be honest with yourself. Is technology taking you away from real everyday life and personal interaction?

*STOP: Time to take some notes!*

Technology is clearly here to stay. How are you using what you hear and see in other people's technology based communication to improve your own? Are you using your technology to communicate with your partner in the same or different ways than you would communicate in person? Are you kind? Are you operating from integrity? Are you using the technology to hide and avoiding critical conversations? Technology use in the form of social media, texting, e-mail, video conferencing is communication — these forms of conversation are here to stay. There is a strong possibility that other technology enhanced communication methods will be invented in the future.

How will you use technology to improve communication in your relationship?

Since my children were born, I have been asking myself, what could conversations look like if we removed smart phones from the landscape? I had my first cell phone before my children were born. I had my first iPhone when my children were ten and eight years old. They have never used a phone with a cord attached to a wall. In their generation, becoming a teen meant getting a personal phone — they really could care very little for owning a car, which used to be the right of passage for teens for so long in America.

Corded rotary dial

I lament and sometimes pine for the pre-phone-in-the-hand-all-the-time-days. I remember when teens — me — had to get up from the table to answer the phone and talk to a friend in front of the entire family! The phone was literally attached to the wall in the kitchen 4 feet from the table! Those days are gone! Teens now walk away from the family or they simply use texting to communicate while pretending to be at the dinner table. Phones are ubiquitous. Phones and technology exist at the dinner table, the bathroom, and everywhere else.

*Random curiosity: Are we the only family that uses the iPad on the toilet?*

I am cool with phone use. I love my phone! Like I said, in 2007 I got my first iPhone and I have carried one ever since! However, from 1995 when I graduated with my communication degree, until now, I cannot even begin tell you how many times I have wondered: "How can I be a part of helping people to continue to interact person-to-person and face-to-face?" I feel like if we do not consciously decide to keep the skills of conversation alive, human interaction and innovation will suffer.

When I see children less than two in a stroller playing on a cell phone or iPad, while a nearby adult converses on another device, ignoring the opportunities to share words about the world with the child, that motivates me to do whatever it takes to keep conversations flowing between people I love! And people like you. When I see entire families texting while eating at restaurants, that keeps me motivated too. My internal motivation for wanting a world with continued face-to-face communication kept me writing this book. When I see couples on a date playing games on their phone instead of talking, I wonder what I could do to help initiate change. Then again, the family or the couple may be playing a phone game together, that's ok, it is their personal time after all.

I am always taking in my surroundings and peripheral conversations. I forget to remind myself that being a conversation vulture does not mean that I understand the conversations I drop in on, because invariably what I pick up will be wildly out of context! Not to mention filtered through my own experiential understanding.

> *Sometimes you have to disconnect to stay connected. Remember the old days when you had eye contact during a conversation? When everyone wasn't looking down at a device in their hands? We've become so focused on that tiny screen that we forget the big picture, the people right in front of us.* — Regina Brett

In my relationship with my husband, and with my children, I accept that modes of conversation are shifting. Grammar is changing. Use of words is in flux. Content is easily searchable. And often, with appropriate use of technology during conversation, the discussions can become richer. Google and similar technologies create a scenario whereby few people are expert anymore. Conversations can be collaborations of shared material that has been collected from the Internet and from each other.

By attempting to not act out while my children repeatedly say stuff like, "Suck My Dick" I allow for the conversation of our family time together to roll forward and continue. I am painfully aware that they hear and see worse information and words in their phone and on endless web searches on a daily basis. What they cannot get on their phone is face-to-face time with me, with my husband, and together as a family (and no FaceTime on a phone is not the same as face-to-face conversation). I intend to create opportunities for as much face-to-face time as possible!

As a family, we have always worked hard to spend a great deal of quality time together during meal times, other times, and at holidays. I expect that future holidays in our home will be full of yet more conversations, insights, and possibly new phrases I'd rather not hear or learn. I see that this younger generation needs to talk. They converse in a different way, often more collaboratively. Often, the iPhone or iPad becomes an added element of the conversation.

My children have taught me that if I can let go of my preconceptions of what a decent conversation will look like, I will invariably get a deeper and more meaningful connection into the lives of those I love. We do not have a rule that says, "No foul language" (we used to, but that has gone to the wayside). We don't say, "Put the cell phone away" unless it is hindering interaction with one another. Rules are broken in our household. Conversations are lively. As a family, we are actively and collectively searching for continued interaction with one another, both verbal and non-verbal and including technology into the equation.

Technology has added a few more dimensions to today's conversations that I feel are worth sharing. Mostly I want to talk about texting. Texting, unlike e-mail, has become a form of talking by typing. Most people would agree that it is easier to send and receive texts than it is to talk on the phone, mostly because you do not have to feel like you are bothering the other person. However, with texting you're chatting in snippets and context can easily be lost. There are all sorts of "rules" for texting that have evolved, just as there are "rules" for direct eye-to-eye conversations.

One thing is for sure, technology is here to stay and I know that what gets created in my lifetime is going to be beyond my wildest imagination. The technology evolution has been huge in the past 50 years! I was born when a single black and white TV existed in our house and was not replaced with a color one for quite a few more years! Then, in college I had my first desktop computer — the Macintosh from Apple Computer!

How has the technology equation affected your relationships?

Take Action. What have my stories about technology made you think about? What funny moments can you think of when technology was the culprit? Would you agree that face-to-face conversation can help people "get more done?" What kinds of rules do you have for yourself about texting, cell phone use or other technology like Skype? What do you think of emoticons? What do you think will be the next BIG innovation around technology and conversations? What are your standby ways of getting off of a technology enhanced conversation? Do you expect immediate responses to your texts from your partner? When is it ok not to respond immediately? What else about technology do you think we should be talking about, but we have not?

*STOP: Time to take some notes!*

Well, we have reached the end of exploring non-verbal communication. I hope you took the time to stop, think, and reflect on the use of touch, other forms of "hearing," body language, writing to communicate, and the technology equation. Next up I am going to help you explore your own internal chatter and other harmful communication patterns.

# Chapter 9 —
# Blame Games: He Said She Said

> Marriage is a mosaic you build with your spouse. Millions of tiny moments that create your love story. — Jennifer Smith

## Play the Game

The blame game: yea, you know the one. He this...she that...it's not fair...it's not right...and so on.

Take Action. We are going to play a game, The Blame Game.

Take any one teeny tiny spec of frustration that you have about your partner. Say for example: he doesn't flush the toilet, or she wears frumpy clothes; he misses the clothes hamper, or she leaves tea ring stains on the kitchen counter; he never puts the toothpaste cap back on the toothpaste, or she leaves her tampons on the back of the toilet all month...do you get the idea here? Think of something that is really nit-picky and, well I want you to think about it, notice it and...

Take one of these teeny tiny daily frustrations and sit with it. Mull the crap over. Fume. Bitch to yourself. Write about it in great detail. Hey, maybe even sit and draw the details of the problem. I mean, really study the situation. Take detailed pictures. Do this for 5 minutes or five days. However long it takes for you to really seriously get to know the stupid shit thing your significant other does that bothers the crap out of you...take the time to really get deeply involved with this frustration you feel.

Now go take a walk. Yes, I said a walk, ok a bike ride, a swim, a yoga class, whatever, get moving and keep thinking about that crappy thing that really irks you. I want you to focus on it as much as you can for a minimum of four hours. Yes, do it!

This little spec of frustration should now be so huge that you think, "This is it! I'm done with this relationship! I cannot live another day like this!" If you are not there yet, study the fucker even more, I want you as mad as hell. This little spec of a frustration is larger than a house or a high-rise. The frustration could fill the Grand Canyon! Great, now you've really done it! You grew a spec of frustration into an insurmountable mountain. So, are you sure? Do you have a clear big visual in your mind of dirty clothes attacking you or tampons dancing in the sky like storm clouds? Well done! Excellent work!

Now, I am going to be...morbid. If your partner died on the way home from work today, what do you think you would miss the most? Sorry to be the bearer of bad news here, but I think you know what I am going to say. Often the stupid, petty, crappy little things operate like tiny stitches in a quilt. Each tiny stitch, that represent daily frustrations, holds together the hundreds of small pieces of fabric. The fabric represents the tiny moments that create your love story and your life together. Together, the stitches and the fabric of life are precious. When the shitty little things are all gone, life, as you know it will begin to tear apart. These shitty little frustrating things are what you will remember when your loved one is gone. The un-flushed poo floater in the toilet — well, I can guarantee you, when the poo is gone, you will miss the whole person!

> Your life is the fruit of your own doing. You have no one to blame but yourself. — Joseph Campbell

I am not saying that you should put up with really bad crap, but honestly, will your world fall apart if the dishwasher is full when you go to bed? Will the relationship wither and die if your partner does not wipe the table off after dinner?

I ask you now, to go a little deeper into this exercise. For a week, go around gathering minute details of awful stuff and treasure them. Maybe even keep a list or a journal. Like those times when a lady bug lands on you — take a minute to count her dots on her back — take the time to notice what bugs you.

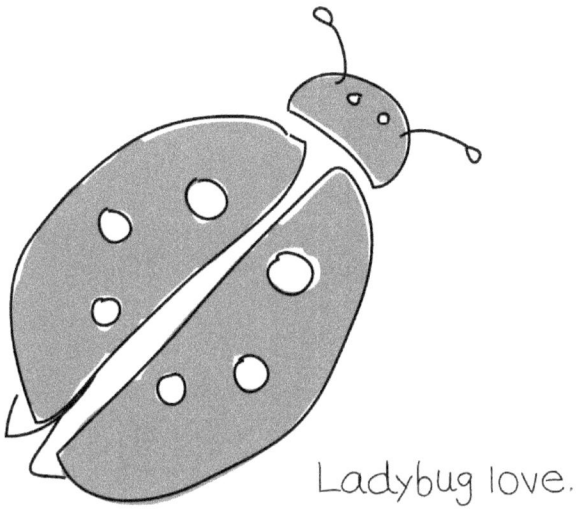

Ladybug love.

Yes, I know you can't wait to try this exercise! You relish keeping a journal of crappy moments, bitter resentments, and stupid stuff you find around the house. Sounds super duper enticing and ridiculous doesn't it? What will happen, or what I hope will happen for you, is that by focusing on and getting a closer look at the things that irk you, you might be able to then get a clearer picture of your own behavior and choices. Our behavior works on a similar level to breathing. Breathing happens, we mostly never think about it — but when we do focus on the breath, then we can expand the breath and fill the lungs. The fuller the lungs the emptier we can get them!

Control of the breath is a yoga thing that I began to learn 25 years ago in a community college class with an excellent instructor who took the time to break down every breath and every pose into the tiniest and smallest of increments so that even a novice could gain control of his or her limbs and lungs. Yoga puts me in the present moment. I get a deep feeling of *now* in my practice. Once I am in the now, I can begin to notice my own behaviors and how they affect my daily existence.

> *Blame is far too prevalent in our world. We blame our parents, our spouses, our employers, our teachers, our government, our upbringing, our environment, and our financial condition (just to name a few). We blame others for our faults and our unhappiness. And every time we do, we lose. Because the decision to blame others for our shortcomings will always keep us from making the changes in our lives that are so desperately needed.* — Joshua Becker

People in relationships must behave and believe in the now, the present moment. Lamenting the past gets you nowhere. Being pissed off for the future ... for example thinking, "I cannot live another day with this shitty sock on the floor" ... is not living in the now — you're projecting to possible future behaviors and beliefs. An additional truth I know about relationships is that we cannot change the behavior of others. We can only change our own behaviors, reactions and actions to the other person's actions. If the sock bothers you right now, pick up the darn thing drop it into the clothes hamper and walk away. Done!

> *Attack the evil that is within yourself, rather than attacking the evil that is in others.* — Confucius

Daily blame games are a stupid waste of time and energy. As soon as you realize that you cannot and do not want to change your significant other, you can free up gobs of time for love, conversation, kisses, and hugs. So go ahead and nitpick the crap out of your partner, on paper, not in person. Get juicy tidbits and record them. Then look at yourself and your own behaviors as well in this way. Be honest. Be truthful. Learn from the data you gather and improve what it feels like to live with you.

You can only control your own reactions to other people's behaviors.

On a related note, you will see remarkable resemblances of behavior and responses to a variety of stimuli in your partner to the people he or she grew up with and was raised by. Banish the tendency to want to compare. Often, comparing your partner to an extended family member does more to hurt than to help. Focus on your significant other and their wonderfulness, and avoid the natural tendencies of judging him or her based on their relatives.

> *Between stimulus and response, there is space. In that space is our power to choose our response. In our response lies our growth and our freedom. — Viktor E. Frankl*

Take Action. There are a few more types of Blame Games that I came up with when writing this book. They are: willingness, non-communication and interrupting. I will go over them in the following sections. But before I do, reflect on your feelings about this first exercise.

*STOP: Time to take some notes!*

Did you do the work or did you simply imagine the work? If you did the work, did the petty stuff make you mad or did you feel a stupid madness in yourself for not taking responsibility for your own rude actions? Did you begin to see the insurmountable annoying behaviors as something to love or something to cherish? If not, what else could be done? Are you ready to take responsibility for your reactions to other people's behaviors? If not, why not?

## Willing

There are ways of being willing to make a thing or a situation between your partner and you better. By "being willing" you can learn to be responsible for your own actions in a situation where you might have chosen to blame your partner. Owning up to your own responsibility in any situation is never easy, but often it is the preferable solution to blaming. Often, "being willing" needs to be addressed in times of anger. When you feel angry, for whatever reason, consider the following:

- be willing to be wrong
- be willing to get help
- be willing to "get out of a rut"
- be willing to kick old habits that no longer serve
- be willing to let go of recycled conversations and arguments

Take Action. What are you willing to change? What are you willing to take responsibility for? What are you willing to ignore? What are you willing to delegate? What other "be willing's" can you think of?

*STOP: Time to take some notes!*

The game of golf is like the idea of "being willing." Golfers hit a tiny white ball hundreds of yards into a tiny hole on a green. Sometimes players hit their ball using the wrong club for the distance. They need to be willing to realize their mistake. Then, they need to be willing to get help, especially when they play a course new to them. The caddy might be a better judge of distance, best club, and best angle for the shot. Even with help, golfers land in water, deep grass, or sand. The correct club and shot will help them out of the rut! An experienced golfer may have picked up habits of play that worked really well when their body was ten years younger, but their aging body requires that they kick old habits that no longer serve. If golfers want to stay in the game they will regularly need to re-up their commitment and shoot for a new handicap, letting go of last years successes or failures!

I encourage you to "be willing" to get into the habit of learning to be a better you, be a better player, and recommit to your relationship.

### Non-Communication

I am going to be brutally honest here. Do not use any of the techniques listed below. Not ever. They are not forms of communication.

1. I can't stand it when you...
2. I wish you would...
3. You always...
4. Sulking, yelling, or storming off.

These phrases say nothing, never work, never will work, and only work to hurt your attempts at communication. Seriously, never...ever....ok. Thanks.

Take Action. Do you commonly use the above forms of non-communication? Be honest, if so, can you attempt to rid yourself of ONE of them for one day? Then, if that's possible, can you go for 21 days, then work on the next hurtful non-communication and so on, until you STOP relying on non-communication.

Yes, this will hurt like crap! You will need to look into the closets, attic, basement, and hiding places inside your mind and heart.

Dig out your own shit and figure out what it is that you are hiding right before you choose these awful non-communication behaviors. The person you love does not deserve your old pain. Comfort yourself and be nice to your partner. How do my harsh words make you feel? Can you challenge yourself?

**STOP: *Time to take some notes!***

This section could quite possibly be some of the hardest work I have introduced in this entire book. Getting rid of non-communication is akin to gambling. You think you might have won, but at what cost? The casinos are in business to make money, not give money. Don't gamble on non-communication; it really is not worth it! Try hard to get rid of non-communication. Your partner and you will be glad of the change. Good Luck!

## Interrupting

Don't interrupt. Don't think or tell the other person what you think they are feeling. Don't even pretend to know that you know what they are going to say. Let your partner get what they want to say out in their own words. Don't "fix" stuff — that's their job — said another way: LISTEN. Don't interrupt.

The reason I feel like this section is an all or nothing proposition is because interrupting leads to misunderstanding. Allowing one person to finish the other person's sentence in mid-conversation is akin to saying, "What you have to say is not important, I can say it better." If one person in the relationship is interrupted more than the other (this is common) then the person being interrupted could begin to feel that their ideas, viewpoints, and concerns are less valid than those of their partner. I, unfortunately, know how this feels, and I also, unfortunately, have caught myself doing the interrupting much more than I care to admit to.

Take Action. For some people breaking this habit will take momentous effort. Go easy on yourself and figure out a way that works for you one day at a time. You gathered the habit of interrupting over a lifetime; do not expect change overnight. What methods have you used before to break bad habits that have worked for you? Try what worked for you before and break the tendency to interrupt. Yes sometimes it means the conversation will take longer. Sometimes it means the conversation will twist towards what you do not want to hear. Do it anyway. No one deserves to be interrupted. Being interrupted feels worse than being ignored.

*STOP: Time to take some notes!*

Interrupting is a hard habit to break. I often catch myself in "interrupting mode." I suppose in some ways the pattern develops due to long histories shared with one another. Unfortunately, that is just another excuse. Interrupting is harmful to clear understanding. Let's think of the habit in this way: interrupting is much like the game Chutes and Ladders. Sometimes you'll find yourself making terrific progress and sliding into harmonious listening. Then, other times you'll be climbing a ladder only to realize that you need to learn not to interrupt all over again. That's ok, like the game, life is about playing and staying the course.

## Warning Signs

As I have said before in this book, I am not a psychologist or licensed marriage therapist, but I do have some personal ideas on what constitutes a "warning sign" in relationships. Warning signs exist in so many different forms. The closer you are to the problem, the less likely that you can see the issue.

I'd like to relate what I mean here to my painting practice. Often when I am painting or drawing if I get stuck on a certain area I need to step back and take in the situation and the image from a different distance, usually from much further back (rather than the arms length at which I paint from). Relationships can work the same way. Sometimes we need to take a giant step back and reevaluate.

Sometimes I do not see the warning signs in my own relationship. Why? Because I am too damn close to it! However, through friends, family, and health professionals I think I have for the most part been able to notice the warning signs when they develop. I have also used techniques such as brief weekends away or trips to go see art alone. When I know I need my brain and heart to mull things over outside of our home, I do myself and our relationship a favor and I get some perspective. When these things are not possible, I go for a really long walk.

The trick is to DO something about your perception of a possible warning sign. Do you act right away or do you sit back and ruminate and wonder if change is worthwhile? Only you can know. I do feel that by sharing common "warning signs" I can at least help you to recognize if any exist in your relationship.

Take Action. Remember, the goal of this book is increased communication and collaboration. What better place is there to deepen communication than to look at adversity and address it head on? Below is the list of Warning Signs I have collected. Can you think of any others? More importantly, can you work together towards solutions and healing?

Warning signs:

1. Being too independent
2. Being selfish (emotional, time, money, etc.)
3. Being jealous

4. Being vengeful
5. Holding grudges and reiterating past mistakes of partner
6. Not talking
7. Not choosing (does mother-in-law or another family member or friend come first, does work come first, does a hobby get more energy than the relationship)
8. Being inflexible
9. Only seeing one side of a situation
10. Lack of romance

If you read this list and think to yourself, "Oh my gosh, I see number 3, 5, 6, and 9..." Stop, take a deep breath and realize that everyone at any time might see some signs and still have a healthy relationship.

I want you to turn the above list around 180°. DO NOT look at the list with your partner in mind. Reread the list with *yourself* in mind. What I am getting at here is: awareness. Can you choose to be more aware of your actions that might look like the above relationship warning signs? Can you choose to work on them? This is NOT about blaming the other person; this is about being a better person. This is about taking responsibility for your own actions. Ok? Please play this game and look deeply at your own behaviors.

*STOP: Time to take some notes!*

Could you take this list and discuss it with your partner? If not, why not? If so, please do. But only after you have become more self-aware. Initially, this is like a game of solitaire. You may win by cheating the cards as you go along, but the sweeter games are the ones that you have won fair and square. You know how to be the best you. No more blame games!

I imagine that the Blame Games Chapter did not feel a whole lot like fun and games. Sorry about that. But we both know that doing the work from this chapter will benefit and beautify the mosaic of your life with your partner. Life is a zillion piece jigsaw puzzle. Not solvable, but fun to put the pieces in one by one, finding the best image. Facing your blaming tendencies head on will make you a better person and partner. So now, let's move on. What other uses of conversation are there?

# Chapter 10 —
# Other Uses of Conversation

> *Let us make a special effort to stop communicating with each other, so we can have some conversation.* — Mark Twain

This book is about relationships, primarily between couples, but invariably couples become a part of other relationships, family members, and the greater public. This chapter looks at how conversations work at a mechanics level. Once couples learn their conversation coping strategies with the person they love, then what they learn can affect and benefit conversatins outside of the relationship.

## Saving Face

In the act of communication there is a natural need and tendency for people to do what is called, "saving face." Basically, this is all about the ego. There are two sides to saving face: one is protecting yourself and the other is protecting the person that you are communicating with.

Let's talk about the first one — protecting yourself. No one wants to feel stupid. No one intentionally sets out to sound stupid or say stupid comments, but shit happens, then you try to back pedal and try to save face! No one tries to do stupid things or forgets to do the stuff we said we'd do, but we do mess up. We all have a deep desire to be liked and respected. When we goof up we try to save face. Saving face does not always work, especially when used in a relationship where two people know each other very well.

The second "saving face" method is often used in an attempt to be polite. Sometimes saving face techniques are used when one person is worried about hurting the other person's feelings. Protecting the other person can be about showing respect through taking the other person's needs and wants into consideration.

Often saving face for yourself or saving face for the person you love means that you are not diving into a crucial conversation. Saving face is like a brick wall. Saving face blocks the potential for intimate connection with your partner. While I do not recommend removing the wall all at once, I do recommend awareness of this communication strategy. Saving face is a strategy, one that you can choose to use, or one that you can choose to pay attention to and gently and mindfully poke holes in or move around into deeper conversations.

Saving face is a relationship tightrope walk with honesty and trust being a huge part of the mix. If you stop protecting yourself, could your partner be better able to understand you? If you stop protecting your partner, can you present information in a loving and honest fashion? Removing the tendency to "save face" in your relationship will take a very very long time, and may never be complete. I do believe that paying attention to incidences of saving face in your relationship can vastly improve the intimacy between you and your partner.

Take Action. Can you think of a time in the past few hours or days where you decided to get mad, get even, or white lie your way out of a stupid place to save yourself from the feeling of humiliation, embarrassment, or some other feeling of inadequacy? Oh, com'on...you know you have, we ALL have at some point or another!

Write down the story that led up to the incident. Write down how things might have been different if you chose honesty and trusted that your partner was able to listen fully to you. Do you need to rely on saving face or are there options and opportunities for growth?

What kinds of tactics have you used to try and cover up a mistake? Has it worked out for you? Does it work better to own up to your blunder and move on?

*STOP: Time to take some notes!*

How about your skills in helping other people to "save face," does this make sense to you? Does the concept seem ridiculous? Do you think that what constitutes saving face is different in different cultures? Are you sometimes extra nice to someone or your partner in order to make the other person feel better? Does this action make them feel better in the long term? Does helping your partner to save face deepen your bond with one another? If your personal integrity includes the value of being honest, is it possible to be honest, be kind and *not* save face for you partner?

## Apologizing

Apologies are tough to navigate. Sure, it can be easy to say, "I'm sorry," but the real apology takes much more conversation savvy and skill. I wonder if some of our skill-less "I'm sorry's" come from misplaced childhood practice. How many times do we see parents saying to their toddlers, "Now, Jack you must say you're sorry, hitting is NOT ok!" or "Jill, give that crayon back to Jack right this minute and say you're sorry!" Then, the little person does as he or she is asked, and moves on. Did the child really feel any remorse for what they did, and did they actually feel sorry? Did they understand what they should feel sorry about? Most of the time, no, they simply did as they were told. We take these blunder skills right into adulthood.

Take Action. I am sure that nearly every week we have something to apologize for that goes unattended to. Did you come home late from work and not call? Did you say you would take care of something and you failed to follow through? Did you say something foolish that you know hurt your partners' feelings, but you cannot figure out the best way to say you're sorry? Did you do something weeks or months ago that you are still feeling remorse for, why haven't you figured out a way to say you're sorry?

**STOP: Time to take some notes!**

Practice the words, "I'm sorry." Face your partner, look your partner in the eye, touch your partner's hand or shoulder and say, "I'm sorry." Use empathy, be in the moment and mean what you say. Typically a *good* "I'm sorry" includes background information and explanation, and a genuine attempt at taking ownership of what you are sorry for. The words, "I'm sorry," said correctly can sometimes make the other person feel better than hearing the phrase, "I love you."

## Forgiveness

Not too long ago one of my children made a big mistake in life. When the event first happened, I was in total shock. I thought I'd never be able to trust my child again. I thought I'd never be able to let him out of my sight until he was 18. I also thought I'd be happy to kick him out of the house as soon as he turned 18! I was angry and confused. What had gotten us to this place? The details do not matter. I doubt that there are any parents of teenagers that cannot relate to the feelings as I have described above. The events leading up to my dismay could be different for every parent, but the reactions may all be similar. In time, I learned how to forgive my son. In time I learned how to say, "I forgive you" to him with complete and utter love and genuine meaning. He is still not 18 as of this writing and forgiveness helped us both move on and grow stronger.

Only one thing can move you and the person you love to a new and beautiful existence together and that is: forgiveness. When you hurt so bad that you feel like you will die, the only remedy is forgiveness. I have some tips for you:

You can forgive without forgetting.
You can forgive without saying that what happened is ok.
You can forgive and still remember.

Forgiveness is about changing your attitude and letting the other person know that you wish them well, that you hope that they, like you, can move on.

Take Action. In close, long-term committed relationships it would be really rare to never have to forgive one another. Do you have a situation in your relationship that could use some "clearing and forgiveness?" Maybe there is a big fat hardship like infidelity or maybe there is a smaller offence looming large? Can you forgive? Do you want to forgive? Can you have this conversation? What can you do to begin healing yourself first? Forgiveness is NOT about expecting changes in the other person. Forgiveness is about adjusting your attitude to the situation. Are you ready to do what it takes? Do you want to do the work? Can you forgive?

*STOP: Time to take some notes!*

I hope that you can find forgiveness in your heart and move forward.

## Promises

I try really hard to keep my promises. For me, keeping a promise is directly linked to my personal integrity. Having said that though, sometimes things happen, decisions are made, and life interferes and I cannot keep a promise. When this happens, I learn to say, "I'm sorry." I also learn to not over-promise. I feel like promises are similar to leaving love notes. When you make a promise, you say that you are going to do something or not do something and then you follow through. What can be more loving than that?

Take Action. Have you made promises that you did not keep or worse that you did not ever intend to keep but you said, "I promise" anyway? What happened? Are there promises that you could offer that could improve your relationship? What are they? What is stopping you from attempting to commit to at least one new promise to your significant other that could enhance your relations with one another? Do you think of a promise as a binding contract or do you idly make promises that you do not intend to keep? If you do not have a full commitment to promises, why not? Where did you learn your behavior? Can you begin to heal and choose to live your life with more integrity towards your word?

**STOP: Time to take some notes!**

In the next week, say the words I promise to your partner for one small thing daily — follow through. Repeat.

## Accepting and Giving Compliments

I adore compliments, but not when it is about my appearance! I feel that what I know and actions that I take are more about who I am as a person. How I look is irrelevant. I would love to get daily compliments on how I handled a tough situation or how I managed my creative work, my work as a chauffeur, cleaner, grocery shopper, the zillion other chores, and a compliment for a hot dinner on the table! Then, when I do get complimented for my actions, I forget to take notice of the compliment! Or I brush it off and say, "Oh, it's nothing, tonight was out of a box!"

Seriously?!? I got what I wanted and then I try to minimize my contribution.

Why do compliments work this way? Why can't we listen and revel in the wonderful words said about us? Could it be that when we get a compliment we then feel like we have to give a compliment in return? Could it be that we hear the same compliment so many times from our partner that the words have lost their luster? I don't know for sure.

Then there is the other side of the compliment component — giving compliments. I'm lousy at giving compliments! I'm fantastic at being nit-picky! My husband has literally learned how to fish for compliments. He says stuff like, "I took out the garbage tonight," or "I finished cleaning the shower, do you want to take a look?" As I write this I have tears in my eyes. Is it sad that he has to do this to get my attention? Or is he so insecure that he needs constant compliments? Who knows! Does it matter? Is it really that hard for me to walk into the bathroom and say, "yeah, wow looks great!" Yes, it is! And I typically will see areas for improvement! Ouch! Yeah, see I told you I am awful at giving and a taking compliments.

Take Action. How about you? Do you regularly give compliments? Do you vary the content of the compliments from appearance to actions, or behaviors and kind gestures? What can you do to accept and notice the compliments you are receiving? Next time you catch yourself about to say something negative, find a compliment instead. The more you practice complimenting, the better you will get. I cannot say more here, I need to go get some proper practice myself! Toodeloos!

*STOP: Time to take some notes!*

A few more things about compliments:

    Make it sincere
    Make it immediate
    Make it unique
    Say it in writing

Most of all…practice accepting and giving compliments.

## Negotiating

Negotiating seems more like a business word to me than a conversation starter or a relationship builder. Yet, in every day situations when we spend time with one another, we are often negotiating. Negotiations are used to find understanding, to create win-win situations, to reach collaboration and yes, even to get what you want!

First, allow me to begin with a note about collaboration in relationship negotiation strategies. When using negotiating tactics, with *collaboration* as the goal, both parties emerge with a solution that fully meets their needs. This is different from *compromise*, where one person is giving something up so that the other person can do what he or she wants. I prefer collaboration, but I will warn you now, true collaboration is not always possible.

My grandparents had a funny arrangement about negotiations in their relationship that lasted throughout their marriage. They would happily joke about their agreement. My grandfather used to say, even after over 50 years of marriage, "we agreed early on in our relationship that she would decide all the little things and I would take care of the big things. So far, there haven't been any big things."

Take Action. Ask each other one question. Who takes care of the little things? How do you negotiate the needs of the individuals and retain integrity of the couple? When and how often are negotiations used to find understanding in your relationship? Do you work to create win-win situations? If not, why not? How often do you reach true collaboration? Do you negotiate to get what you want more often than you should or not often enough?

*STOP: Time to take some notes!*

Oops, that was more than one question!

## Strategizing

Oh, bother...here is another business term! Why did I put this in here? For one, I think we can comfortably say that this book is one big huge strategizing planning tool! Great, now that we have that clear I want your word that you will use the contents in this book to work together. For me, strategizing has some negative connotations, like, "hum, how can I get out of..." or "If I do such and such, I might be able to get her to do such and such..." These are the possible negative uses of strategizing. To get what you want for *you*, without adequately considering what is best for the partnership. This is not a long term win-win solution!

Please focus on the positive uses of strategy! Move your relationship forward with grace, dignity and love.

*STOP: Time to take some notes!*

Take Action. Make a plan for how and when you will continue to use Conscious Curiosity and the ideas and exercises to strengthen your relationship. Create a strategy.

## Terms of Endearment

My guess is that very few relationships exist without terms of endearment. Why we use such silly names is a mystery to me. However, terms of endearment can also be like a noose; maybe one person has outgrown their fondness of the term that they keep getting called. Keep in mind, terms of endearment are highly dependent on the situation they are used in, such as tone of voice, body language, and social context — all stuff we have addressed in this book. But still, the terms such as Honey Boo, Babe, Pumpkin, Lemon Pie, My Love, Mia Bella, Sweetie, Hot Shot, and Pookie may all find their way into your conversations with your partner. Notice them. Decide for yourselves the importance of such terms.

*STOP: Time to take some notes!*

Take Action. Have some fun. Make a long list of some funny terms of endearment that you have heard others use. Think of your parents, grandparents, and other couples you know and admire, what do they call each other? Think back on any terms you have called each other, why did you stop or why do you still use the terms? Talk about times that you would rather NOT have your partner use your special terms of endearment. Talk about times when you wish you did have terms of endearment, for example as a part of sexual encounters.

## Report vs. Rapport

At the end of a busy day, you sit down to dinner and you start to talk. At least I hope you understand by now the importance of stopping to check in each day! There are options available to you about how you share your day. You can "report" your day in a dry matter of fact way, like the news. The conversation remains in reporting mode unless your partner chooses to get animated and asks\ you questions and prompts you for more information along the way. Rapport refers to the attempt at making meaning and creates connection and understanding through conversation. Communication with rapport is usually known and felt by both parties, they have a feeling of a harmonious give and take and a flow to the conversation.

We already talked about listening and key strategies to being a better listener. Rapport happens when both people are good conversationalists and excellent listeners. Rapport is a beautiful skill to develop. Most of the skills outlined in this book coupled with the hundreds of questions created to enrich understanding can or will develop rapport between you and your partner.

I do not feel rapport with my spouse during *every* conversation, I think it would be foolish to think that we can have smooth flowing conversations all of the time. However, when conversation begins to feel like we are only reporting to one another on a regular basis, I try to take stock and consider what it is that I can do to improve matters and re-establish rapport.

### STOP: Time to take some notes!

Take Action. Consider the differences between regular reporting and having rapport in conversations. Do you want to shovel information at your partner or do you want to bond with your partner? Do you want to establish connection or simply relay information? BOTH types of conversational style can play a vital role in your communication. The first step is to recognize the differences. The second step is to work towards choosing the best mode for the conversation at hand. Do you think it really matters whether you are using a reporting style of conversation versus attempting to establish rapport? Discuss your thoughts on this topic.

## Confusing Speech

We all know what confusing speech sounds like. In order to minimize confusing speech I have one piece of advice:

*Talk slowly and think quickly.*

Confusing speech can happen so quickly and so very often. I am afraid to write about it because aren't we all confused much of the time when conversing? Can we really ever know what the other person fully meant? For me to help you to understand this, I will go back to my art skills. No two people ever see the same color the same way. All of us have retinas that work in our unique way with our past as the foundation for color viewing. Blue comes in many colors, and your blue is very likely different from your partners blue. That is the reality of how color works in the brain.

We can literally say one thing that we feel is a statement of fact, when in reality our partner may totally miss the mark and hear or understand our phrase differently. Don't believe me? Then you have not been looking for these subtle and confusing speech moments. We are lucky when what happens as a result of what we have said makes the confusing speech instantly recognizable. But, this is not always the case.

Confusing speech will always be a part of any conversation; however being aware of the existence of perceptions of stories and statements *never* being identical in each other's minds can help each person in the relationship to be slightly more empathetic.

**STOP: *Time to take some notes!***

Take Action. Talk slowly and think quickly. Consider the shared history between you to help form a story around something complex that you are attempting to share. Try speaking in a way that the other person knows that you are attempting to share the information with cues or details that they will understand. Lower your tone of voice or speak with a smile. Understand that you can never eliminate all confusion, but you can reach for clearer understanding.

## Conflict

Do we really want to talk about and create conversation around the idea of conflict? No, not really. Could it be that conflict can be resolved by working on your conversation skills. No, not really. Conflict between people is normal. Conflict is healthy. Conflict can solve problems when two people decide to "fight fairly." Is there any way to really fight fairly? No, conflict never feels like the best situation to be in while you are going through the conversation.

Keep in mind that you DO go through the conversations you have in your life! There is a beginning, middle, and an end to all conflicts. No conversations need to be forever. Conflict should not be about wallowing in an argumentative stage. Rarely can two people who care about each other and who respect each other stay in conflict for very long. However, a very long time is a relative state. You'll want to work your way towards a solution.

*STOP: Time to take some notes!*

Take Action. So, you don't like the word conflict? And you don't like being in the midst of conflict? Who does? Do you think of conflict, as my husband does, and say to yourself or others, "We're not arguing, we're just talking!" Be that what it may, conflict does exist and so do many other names for the concept of conflict, such as: dispute, quarrel, squabble, disagreement, dissension, clash, and so on...what other words can you think of? Have you discovered paths to resolving conflict that seem to work for both of you? What are they? Lastly, how can you resolve to move through conflict as a natural part of conversation, rather than wallow in it?

# Chapter 11 —
# Passion, Mission, and Vision

> *I think the best thing for you to do is just live your life. Live a life that's worth living, one where you do what you want to do, pursue your passions. That way, if you meet someone, they'll be joining a life that's already really good.* — Dan Savage

## Create Your Own Blueprint

For many of us, myself included, living life means following prescribed societal norms. You do this, then that, and then this happens. Then the expectations mount...until you realize, shit, this is not what I wanted for myself or my relationship! Most of this book is about using conversations to unravel and reveal the real dreams within you. I hope, the dreams for BOTH of you. You can create your own blueprint. You can create the life you want to live. I am not going to tell you that the path to your most authentic life will be easy, unfortunately it will not be. I can totally promise you rough spots along the way! However, the journey not taken is going to be far more painful.

Are you ready to create your own blueprint?

All right, so seriously have you ever considered what the difference is between passion, mission, and vision? Here is how I see it: passion involves your emotions and having an excitement about doing something, mission involves leadership and bringing the best of you to others, vision is about your ability to see your dreams for the future and/or what you want to envision and create as your legacy.

> *Ubuntu. I am; because of you. People are not people without other people.*

Take Action. Here we go again into a slew of questions. Are you ready?

Passion — dig deep into your emotions here. What makes your soul sing?

Mission — What do you find yourself always wanting to tell other people? What do you see in the world that makes you mad enough to make change?

Vision — Create a legacy. What needs to happen to create a legacy of your liking?

Ha-ha I teased you, that's it for the questions in this chapter! You see, I think that maybe, since you've already done so much probing throughout this book, this chapter can flow out of you beautifully. Don't hold back. This is your life map and blueprint. Create the life you want to live.

**STOP: Time to take some notes!**

I suggest you take some scratch paper, exquisite paper, and a special pen and go outside to create the words for your Passion, Mission, and Vision. Write and rewrite your ideas on scratch paper until the words feel and sound great to you. Make your passion, vision, and mission statement beautiful, kind, and full of life. Then write the words on exquisite paper. Maybe words alone feel like they are not enough. Ok, then draw and doodle your way to your most authentic life. Use crayons if you like!

Extra credit. Create a couples Passion, Mission, and Vision statement. Use all of the conversation starter techniques and skills you have developed this far to make this happen.

Double extra credit. Support your partner as much as possible to fulfill their Passion, Mission, and Vision. What better loving gift is there than to support and encourage someone you love? Help each other grow and make dreams come true.

# Chapter 12 —
# Continue the Journey

> Most people get married believing a myth that marriage is a beautiful box full of all the things they have longed for: companionship, intimacy, friendship, etc. The truth is that marriage at the start is an empty box. You must put something in before you can take anything out. There is no love in marriage. Love is in people. And people put love in marriage. There is no romance in marriage. You have to infuse it into your marriage. A couple must learn the art and form the habit of giving, loving, serving, praising keeping the box full. If you take out more than you put in, the box will be empty.
> Quote found on Facebook, The Santa Claus page.

## What is in Your Love Box?

I bet you feel like you were bombarded with questions throughout Conscious Curiosity! Well, you were! Through my ceaseless probing and your relentless pursuit of answers, we built a communication, collaboration and cash (potential) toolbox, um...love box! Yep, you didn't know it, but I have been helping you to have a full love box for relationship success.

I know, I called this book Conscious Curiosity and I mentioned communication, collaboration, and cash, and...I asked you to work on your mastermind project, and... I called the work a quest for passion, mission, and vision writing. I even called it a book for creating connection through communication. All of Chapter 5, Trophy Relationship or Real Relationship, presented conversation starters. But really through it all, I had a goal for you. I wanted you to fill your love box.

This chapter is all about looking at what you already have, adding what you want and getting rid of what is not working in your relationship. So, what does you box look like now? What do you want it to look like?

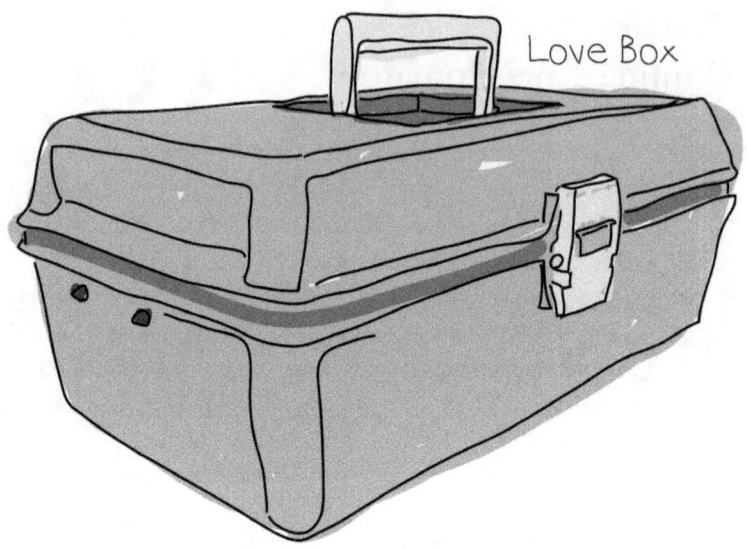

Take Action. What did you put into your love box? Take a moment to jot down the top five things that you can carry with you that you did not have before you read Conscious Curiosity and did the work as outlined in this book. Maybe you are listening better? Maybe you are spending more time together? Hopefully you are kissing each other more frequently? I dream of you looking forward to joy in your next year(s) together! Do you find yourselves asking each other great questions with more frequency? What's different? Name your five love box favorites.

*STOP: Time to take some notes!*

Maybe doing all the work in this book has been really hard and eye opening. Maybe you feel like you could use more help. Would you be willing to read other books together and seek professional help in an area of your relationship that needs growth? Why or why not? Do you think there is such a thing as a relationship that can stay the course — that just is — or do you believe in constant need for life adjustments both forward and backward? Talk about this idea.

Your love box has been in storage mode. I want you to go and open the box now, gather, sort through, examine, and cherish the contents.

## What More Can You Add?

Are you one of those over-achieving couples? Maybe you have been working like crazy people, having loads of fun and thus created a pro-love box? Great! If you were able to build a pro-love box, what's in it? Are there more than 20 new tools and skills for success? Yeah? Write them down. Hooray for you!

I am one of those creative people who absolutely adores fancy new gadgets and specialized tools to help make projects perfect. For example, using a hammer and a nail is not enough to hang a painting. I have to have a pencil, measuring tape, electronic leveling gadget, super fine specialized hanging nails, step stool, hammer, and well, you get the idea, I like lots of the right tools and gadgets to get the job done!!

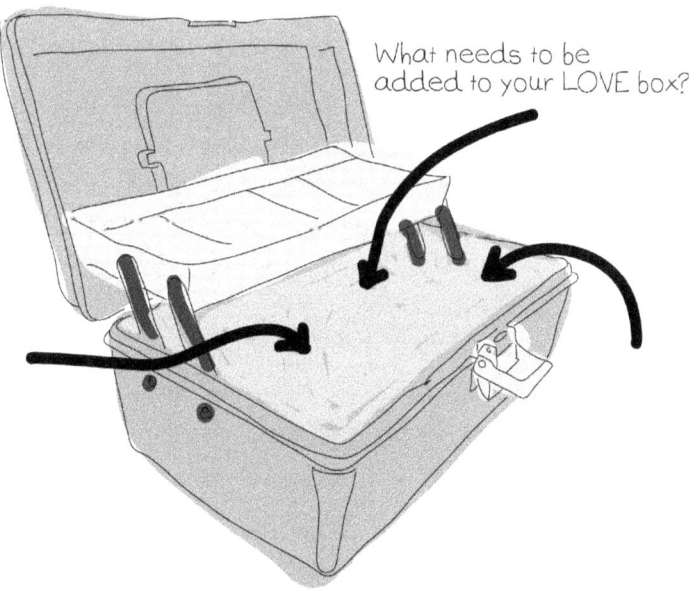

What needs to be added to your LOVE box?

Similarly to how I work as an artist, I tried to make this book chock full of tools and gadgets for building successful relationships while using conversation as a way to initiate communication and collaboration.

*STOP: Time to take some notes!*

As you know, I believe that with a full love-box your cash flow will increase as well! Has your cash flow changed? If so, how and why? What else needs to be done in this area? Go through the table of contents to refresh your memory. What tools have you added to your love box throughout the journey we have shared?

Adding to you life is not enough; there is also need for removal of what's not working. We'll look at this topic now.

## What Needs to be Removed?

Wait a minute! Once in a while any good toolbox gets overfull or worse the tools break down and are no longer serviceable. Unfortunately they take up space in the treasured box.

Has this happened to you in your relationship? Do you keep using old tools that are no longer servicing your relationship? Do you do certain things in a way that really could be done better with the new tools you learned while reading and testing new ways of communicating? What needs to be removed?

*STOP: Time to take some notes!*

What underling rules are a part of your relationship that are no longer servicing your relationship? What are you taking for granted that needs to be recognized? What are you doing that is no longer helpful? How can you come up with new paradigms? What rules need to be broken or better yet discarded?

Let go of all that's not working.

If you cannot think of what to remove or change in your relationship, try this question. In the spirit of my SMD_LMP story, what event has happened in your life that you would *never* share on Facebook? What event is too horrifying or embarrassing to share with me, even though I shared a whole lot here with you?

How about what would you never tell your parents, but it really did happen in your relationship? What would you never ever tell your grandparents? Remove the power of this event, talk about it with one another, and find the humor. Talk about it and take it out of your love box. Bury the treasure. Toss the garbage from your relationship were it belongs in the trash. Let it go. Remove whatever is not working and create room for love and beauty.

## Plan to Celebrate

Please remember to CELEBRATE YOUR GROWTH!

I hope you enjoyed this journey in building skills for relationships. I hope you had tons of fun flexing your conversation muscles. In using communication and collaboration through listening, uncovering truth bombs, conversation starters, mastermind work, numbers work, non-verbal communication, playing the blame game, analyzing the Pandora's box of the many other uses of conversation, and creating your passion, mission, and vision statements, you must have learned a little something wonderful about your partner and yourself.

> *A successful marriage requires falling in love many times, always with the same person.* — Mignon McLaughlin

I know I enjoyed thinking about how millions (I can keep dreaming, can't I?) of couples would use this information while I was writing. Each time I got stuck I would think about another person that I might be able to help. That got me excited and I would sit down again and write and write. I kept writing, I kept writing in the same way that I keep waking up each day and choosing to be married.

> *Being married is about making the choice to make your marriage work, to communicate and to be willing to be vulnerable while giving of yourself one day at a time.*

Choosing the path of being married sounds antiquated at times. But a marriage or partnership does not have to be stifling or horrid, you can write your own rules...be sure to do this together. Here is the reminder again, communication, collaboration and cash with lots of faith mixed into the day to day.

# Celebrate!

I know that being married for 50 years, like my parents are, is not very sexy these days. I also realize that saying and hearing Suck My Dick and Lick My Pussy at the dinner table is not very sexy either, especially when in the company of one's own children! What do I mean by sexy? Desirable — Attractive — Exciting! However, I would like to see a time when good communication and dream sharing is sexier!

We currently live in a throw away society. Bottled water is sexy! Single use plastic is rampant. In the United States people regularly replace their car every three years or less. Cell phones become "outdated" every 18 months or less. How we treat our stuff is translating into how we treat the people we love. Relationship roundabouts seem commonplace. Divorce is common. However I believe having the qualities of desirability, attractiveness and excitement does not have to be through away! Let's think of "in it for the long haul" as being sexy, shall we?

> While writing this book I found out that the divorce rate in the area where I live is 66%. Holy moly that is an awful number!

I find the divorce rate and the action of moving towards divorce itself amongst people to be very sad for everyone. Mostly, I cannot even begin to imagine how hard and awful a divorce must be. My heart cries out for children of divorce. Could it be that by taking responsibility for our own actions and behaviors we could reach a point when we all take better care of one another? For me, the people I love are so much more important than stuff. So much so, that I took a year of my life to share this book with you.

Of course I shouldn't be comparing stuff to people. No one would admit to throwing away a partner. That is too awful to imagine, there are feelings and investments in time and trust. But the thing is, are we taking enough time to nurture the people we love? Do we have important and mundane conversations more than we drive, shop, or work? Only you can know this for your own relationship.

I also cannot imagine how lonely our world must feel, when taken on alone, without close relationships, with so much data and change as a regular part of life, but that's me. How about you? Are you ready to continue starting and sustaining conversations as a priority in your life?

If you have read this far and attempted even only one Take Action step in this book, I am so pleased for you. I hope you do more. Celebrate each step of the way. Hug more often. See each other through the lenses of love and joy.

If you have done much more than one action step or one crucial conversation then celebrate a little bit bigger. If you're like me, and you have poured over the ideas in this book and made lasting, critical changes in your relationship, do yourself a favor, celebrate even bigger!

My husband and I have not had a vacation together without the children since they were born. Sure, we have had a few short weekends here and there — we sent them away to the grandparents and we stayed at home. But this year we are getting on a jet and traveling to a new place that interests us and we are exploring new possibilities for a whole week together. I know, many people raise kids and take far more holidays than we ever did, but this is our Celebration. What will you do to celebrate?

PS. We're back! The Celebration was even better than expected.

## From My Heart to Yours

I wrote this book from my heart. All I know and all I could write about are reflections on my daily attempt to find joy in my relationship with my husband and my family. Through finding my joy, abundance, and beauty I wrote with the hope that I could share my wealth of gratitude. I have not always felt the gratitude I am feeling as I write this conclusion. At times, the conditions of marriage and motherhood have felt like a ball and chain and constricting, like a giant boa. I am not kidding! I can tell you from my daily experience that marriage is harder and more challenging than I ever expected. Being a parent is constricting, time consuming, energy zapping, and more.

Over twenty years ago, when I made a promise to my husband to be the stay-at-home parent for our children, I never could have foreseen how I would feel over 20 years later. I never could have foreseen how much technology (even though I worked in The Silicon Valley at Cisco Systems at the time) would change everything about how my life would operate, feel, and look like on a daily basis. I did not know that ramping back into the workplace at the level I was at would be pretty near impossible. I did not know that I would miss out on workplace friendships and connections. However, I was following my heart. Raising my children with me at the core of their solid foundation kept coming up as being the most important thing to do. I felt this way deep down, even when I felt me slipping away under the guise of giving to them. I was following my heart even when I dearly wished to contribute my varied passions in the every day world.

I have actually had people tell me, to my face, that I have not felt pain. Many tell me that I was lucky to be able to stay at home. I was lucky to be with my children daily but as far as others understanding my pain, I respectfully disagree. Who are they to judge my pain? Impossible. Can any of us measure each other's pain? No. We each do what we do. I have done what I felt called to do. Often I did what I felt was best for the family, not for myself. In so doing I was taking responsibility as an adult to live the life I chose to live. For better or for worse...

Often when I did what I felt was right I was in pain deep inside myself. I often wondered. Have I shared my biggest and best strengths with the world? Maybe not, but maybe I have. My pain comes from wanting to do more outside of the walls of our home. My pain comes from wanting to share more of me and to broadcast the ideas I hold dear. My pain comes from not knowing how to offer what I know to the world.

I believe that all people need the opportunity to share their biggest strengths and gifts with the world. My children are about to launch into the world to learn how to share their biggest strengths and gifts. My older child already has a job and he is beginning to know what his gifts are. My younger son is working as a camp counselor during the summer and he is finding his way through high school. Both of them find continued community in the schools that they have chosen. Both of them have much to learn and many forks in the road ahead. They will be able to chose their own path. I am excited to witness their continued journey.

> There are two ways to think about kindness. You can think about it as a fixed trait: either you have it or you don't. Or you could think of kindness as a muscle. In some people, that muscle is naturally stronger than in others, but it can grow stronger in everyone with exercise. Masters tend to think about kindness as a muscle. They know that they have to exercise it to keep it in shape. They know, in other words, that a good relationship requires sustained hard work.
> — Emily Esfahani Smith

My journey has been what it is because of the choices I have made. I am blessed to have been able to share so much of my life with my two wonderful boys. I am blessed to have had a husband and family who believed in the traditional role of a wife and mother.

These blessings gave me room to look at what it means to Suck My Dick and Lick My Pussy in the public forum of this book. In the end, there is no sucking and licking, what I found was my conscious curiosity, my constant questioning. How can I make marriage more fun and lasting for others, and for myself? How can I bring the idea of personal responsibility to the forefront? How can I help the world to be a kinder gentler place? How can I help people to understand that communicating to connect works?

When using the words or acronym SMD becomes a regular way of communicating in a relationship, there could be a problem. There is very likely a lack of genuine kindness and respect. But maybe the opposite is true; by continuing the conversation we are deepening the intimacy and connection with those we love.

The blessings in my life have given me a chance to learn what it is that I needed to share on a larger scale. I needed to share how much I value a world with better communication and creativity. I am fortunate to have been able to hone in and really study this topic while living in a loving committed relationship. I am walking the talk. I can also honestly say, I am not perfect and things are not always glorious and wondrous.

The writing for this book began from pain. I am the dreaded "white bread" that I spoke of elsewhere in this book. Unfortunately, I do not want, nor did I ever really want to be known as, "just a wife and a mom." I never did and yet I somehow managed to make a commitment to the role and my husband was witness to that commitment. Our families too, were and are in large part supportive and even insistent of keeping me in the role of wife and mother.

Yet, my kids knew at a very early age that I was living a daily struggle. I often sacrificed me to be there for them. They would point out my conflicted state. They would patiently say at the end of a school day — "mom, did you paint today? If you didn't, you should!" or "You're being crabby, do you need to spend time in your studio?" Children are better than mirrors, because unlike the inanimate object, they really can and do talk back even when I never dared ask, "Who is the fairest of us all?" or better yet, "what is my role, and were are my talents and strengths most needed?"

This book is one of many steps I have taken to unzipping what I felt I needed to do to build a stronger relationship with my life partner. I also needed to figure out a way to move forward with my relationship, instead of out of it. Yes, that is real. I have decided day after day to stay *in* the relationship and try to keep the little bits of me from disappearing into a black ocean of pain.

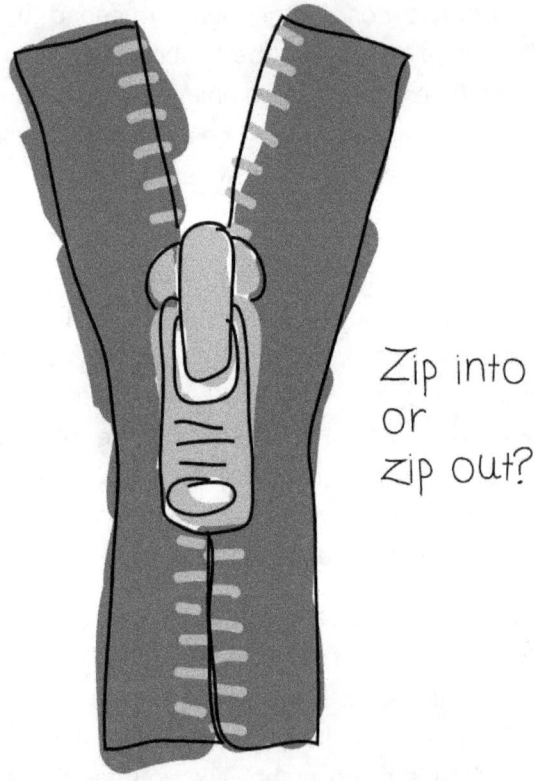

Zip into or zip out?

For years I have created paintings, written words, and kept on sketching what I saw happening around me. All the time knowing that if I could just keep the creator in me alive, all would not be lost. I knew that one day I would create something big to share. This book is one bigger thing. I am beginning to feel sure there is more to come.

The more I worked on this book the more I began to think that after food and shelter, my relationship to my husband and my family falls really high on the spectrum of, "That which is most important to me in my life." In the fast paced reality of life today, intellectually, we can say that our relationships are *really* important, but physically, mentally, and emotionally in everyday life are we honestly giving our relationships our best effort? I am not sure we are.

For the most part I would argue that I have, but when I do a deep cleaning, so to speak, and look at the details the way that I did as I wrote this book, I now see so many areas that are in need of improvement. One place to begin is to pay attention to my spouse, to look up and make eye contact and acknowledge him when he enters a room or when he attempts to engage with me in conversation. Sure I have felt "stuck" and "rudderless" and emotionally distraught. Who hasn't? We all have choices as to how we act and use our time towards what is most important to us.

> *Just as human beings have a basic need for food and shelter, we also have a basic need to belong to a group and form relationships.* — Emily Esfahani Smith

Life is best in conflict. Spending time with those I love and spending time nurturing the beautiful, sensitive, creative soul within me. They are both important. The conflict builds character in me, makes me stronger and wiser.

Like I said, I had times that I did not want my ball and chain and constricting boa holding me in the place of wife and mother. Maybe the roles of wife and mother should have been enough, for many women they are enough. Yet for me, they were not and are not enough, not even close. There are many times of constraint and pain. Maybe there could have been a little less pain if I had been able to create a Mastermind plan with my husband before we had children...who knows! Lord knows we tried at the Engaged Encounter!

Maybe there could have been a little less pain if I could have found my voice earlier, but I was busy. Busy raising my children (with no extended family nearby) and nurturing my relationship to my husband in the best ways I knew how. I was also busy growing up and growing into my sense of self. Slowly I was beginning to learn to trust the wisdom and intuition inside of me. I am continuing to work on believing in the ideas inside of me, learning to nurture me, and learning to reach outside of the home for what I need and want in life — including what I want to offer to others outside of the home.

Today I can joyfully say, the challenge and the pain of the roles I have played is outweighed by the love, compassion, hugs, and general feeling I get from being a part of a legacy of family members who choose to stay married and committed to those they love. I do feel a horrible pressure in my role in our family. Pressure to not be the one to actually fuck up... or step out... or make mistakes...

Knowing there are so many deeply committed relationships in *my* family makes me crazy sometimes! Proud at other times. Curious with wonder, often. Why us? Why our family? Why can't others find peace, love, kindness, forgiveness, and beauty in their relationships? And then again, how do my family members navigate long-term marriages behind closed doors. Where is the truth? What are they doing that works? I have no idea...

How does one family produce so many married couples? I don't know. I am not an inside observer of what goes on behind their closed doors.

I was and am able to do one thing.

I was and am able to look inside my own private life. I combed through ideas, experiences, and private moments. I am risking putting our experiences into the public realm in the form of this book. Why? To share. I worked hard to find and know my inner voice. I choose to let it shine in hopes that I can help others to shine as well…

I hope that others too, can find the courage to grow into deeper love in their relationship, instead of out. I believe this: All you need is communication, collaboration, cash, and a huge amount of faith…

*Build your own loving partnership using conscious curiosity.*

*Take the time to communicate to connect.*

Conscious Curiosity came from the deepest wells of what I have to offer. My wish for you, dear reader is that you may live your days in the challenge of being a better you in partnership with your loved one. I thank you for reading and I welcome your feedback. Thumbs up to you!

# Chapter 13 —
# Meal Times at Our House

> My idea of a good night has always been having a lovely meal and a proper conversation. — Kirsty Gallacher

Meal Times at Our House is a story of how the spark of an idea led to this book. This chapter also includes the reasons I kept writing this book, even when I felt like I never would finish.

## How SMD_LMP Came About

The words: "Suck My Dick" became a refrain in our household during Thanksgiving Holiday 2013. Much to my dismay, Suck My Dick or SMD punctuated every conversation. You see we, my husband and I, are the parents of teenage boys. This particular year, the phrase "Suck My Dick" or the acronym SMD, was being said, before dinner, during dinner, after dinner, and basically the whole entire weekend holiday. SMD punctuated conversation in much the same way periods are used in conventional writing.

> I could not stop nor control the use of the phrase SMD. For a few days the experience was unfortunate and sad, for me.

I was not the one saying: Suck My Dick. I was the person listening to the words, as if they were a normal part of conversation! I was the one who felt like I was being force-fed a huge banana or even a watermelon that I was not hungry for! In this book, I am not advocating the use of words such as Suck My Dick in regular normal every day conversation. However, I DO want to advocate the art of conversation. And on occasion that might mean learning to enjoy conversations in whatever form they take! Allow me to explain.

The Suck My Dick refrain really bothered me. Talking and using these types of phrases is not how I raised my children! Yet, here I was listening to Suck My Dick as if it was a legitimate form of conversation and daily speech. So I suppose, this is exactly how I raised my children. We get what we create and tolerate, right?

At one point I blurted out, "Lick My Pussy!" as a period to one of many statements, during a more lively part of our family conversation that included the use of the Suck My Dick refrains. I wanted to see if adding to the mix of atrocities would shut them up! Instead, they laughed.

"Mom, that's not ok..." they said, "Mom, eewww..." They believed that what they were saying was perfectly acceptable! Yet, when I tried to interject a new form of the same idea I was counter productive. I was shot down.

Except not really, because now some of the charge of the words had dissipated. We all began laughing instead of trying to make the situation seem serious and wrong. The conversations continued and we shared stories of the past several months, stories of past holidays, and conversed about plans for future events together as a family. Another words the conversation was allowed to flow and grow.

I am not advocating foul language. I am asking couples to determine their priorities. What is more important to you behind closed doors in a private family gathering? Do perfect manners count? Or do laughter, communication, and sharing memorable moments matter most? Only you can know for sure in your own personal situation.

A day later, while Suck My Dick was still popular in our household meal conversations and I was getting a little wiser, I said, "You know, someday, I will put those words on the cover of a book and publish the book."

The table went quiet.

The boys even stopped moving. Boys, you may know, never stop moving.

"You wouldn't?!?" said J.

"Um, she's an artist and she writes a blog and she does say weird things in public…ah, umm. Would you really Mom?" says C.

A bit more quiet and stillness abound around the table.

The husband, Derek, chimes in, "Who would buy a book with a title like that?"

Pause…head tilt…smile…

"On second thought, maybe lots of people would!"

You are holding the book in your hands: SMD_LMP! (But I changed the title to Conscious Curiosity during the final edit in order to reach a wider audience.) As you have undoubtedly become aware, this book is a guide for increasing communication skills and conversations between people in committed relationships. The exercises were chosen to build on pre-existing communication strategies and skills. The work was intended to create opportunities for renewed interest in your relationship. The conversations will likely create room for new stories in your life together.

You may be thinking, that you'd like to have more control over the course of conversations in your relationship. You might be wondering why I kept "allowing" my children to talk the way they did. You might be wondering why I did not walk out, or punish them. Moving in the moment and staying present with the family was far more important to me at the time. Being and feeling within the moment was a far superior joy than trying to control to conversation. So, can you relate? Do you want more control over conversations in your family? Maybe you do, but maybe I can change your mind. I thought I wanted more control too!

Possibly the idea of having more control over serious conversations prompted you to pick up this book. I certainly wanted to control and STOP the words and acronym for Suck My Dick from flowing so freely for a whole weekend! Until I took a breath, looked around the table and realized that simply being with these marvelous creatures that I call family was loaded with possibility and beauty.

I'd love to tell you that this book will give you a ton of information on how to control conversations, but clearly, that has not been my strength! My growth as a parent and as a wife has been through letting go of preconceived notions of what it means to be a wife and mother. I have tried my best, and that's all I have to offer. The best of me has come through listening, learning, and being patient.

> When you realize you've made a mistake, take immediate steps to correct it.

I tried to soften or shed my imagined or real ill conceived beliefs around what it means to "be a good wife and mother." What I wanted to control became less important to me than the shared intimacy that developed through communication and stories around the dinner table. I have also learned we need to lighten up and allow life to unfold, including awful dinner conversations and even more, to stop regretting the shoulda, coulda, woulda moments!

In the end, I realize, I do not want to control the outcome of my life with my husband and family. My values have shifted over time — thanks in big part to conversations around the dinner table. What I want for my relationship with my husband requires that I let go of control. Control, or making life into what I think is right, is stagnant and a recipe for the death of us. I'd rather have LIFE!

This may sound like I am contradicting the Mastermind planning that I have advocated for in this book (Chapter 6). There is, however, a subtle yet important difference. I want life to unfold beautifully, as it is supposed to. I want life to teach me and I wish to learn to live as if each moment is precious. At the same time, if I ignore the work of Mastermind Planning what can happen is I do not create room for opportunity. What can happen is more of the same of what has not worked well for us as a couple and as a family.

How can I explain this? In each moment I give up control and live as much as possible in the moment. I appreciate the beauty of any given breath, word, sound, smell, and movement. I am one of those people who stops regularly to pick up a rolly-polly bug on my morning walk. I watch birds fly from tree to tree. I watch water sparkle under sunlight. I sit and admire the banter of communication between my boys at the dinner table.

The Mastermind planning is about putting my husband and myself in the best circumstances for living this nuanced life. People often wonder why we have moved so much as a couple; I think it all boils down to the contradiction I am attempting to explain here. Life is not given to us to give up and live in the status quo. Life is given to us to live fully with joy and beauty. For us, maybe more especially for me, there has been quite a lot of exploring to find the life worth living.

In letting go of control, I invite beauty and goodness.

I want love, laughter, and life. I want kindness and gentleness to prevail. I want deep connection with the people I love and the planet I live on. I hope you do too.

## A Golden Wedding Anniversary In Our Family

A golden wedding anniversary served as my muse in my desire to share my ideas on communication for couples in this book. I have felt called to write this book ever since our SMD Thanksgiving. So, I wrote and researched for a year. Then, my parents learned of this book when I was doing what I thought would be the final editing. Sadly, they were appalled at my original title. They would not even digest one chapter. I almost gave up on the project.

Something deep inside me insisted that I persist. In the end, I decided that my parents would not want me to keep my ideas and the content in this book secret and unshared. I knew I could not live with myself if I shelved the idea, the content, and the genuine need to bring this project to completion.

I know my parents love me. I love them with all my heart. I will risk their dismay with my word choices and correlations of communication and conversation to the sexual act of fellatio that I wrote about in this 76,000+ word book. I am fairly certain, in time, they will understand why I left the foul language in the stories (but I did change the title).

> *If you bring forth what is within you, what you bring forth will save you. If you do not bring forth what is within you, what you do not bring forth will destroy you.* — Jesus Christ

They celebrated 50 years together in June 2014. They clearly understand the importance of communication and commitment. From my vantage point they have remained beautifully married for 50 years. I continue to see mutual respect and love sparks between them.

Their party invitation for their 50th stated that they wished to celebrate "50 Years of Mutual Misunderstandings" with us, the guests. How's that for an insightful or a really stupid love statement! To me mutual misunderstanding is like saying, "I give up!" "I don't want to understand." Or to phrase an overused term: "Whatever."

I wonder if they know that the Urban Dictionary has defined Mutual Misunderstandings as, "an event that can occur when two or more people have a conversation about something mutually understood to both individuals, yet neither needs to (or can) explain it."

To me, Mutual Misunderstandings is like announcing that mutual assumptions create an atmosphere of common knowledge that may very well be incorrect information. I hope to some degree they understood the humor in their proposition of celebrating "mutual misunderstandings." By celebrating mutual misunderstandings, they are basically agreeing that when two people know each other too well they risk not knowing each other at all. I cannot know for sure if this is what they meant. But I still find mutual misunderstanding a curious way to celebrate 50 years.

Maybe 27 years from now I will have a different perception of "mutual misunderstandings" with my husband!

In any case, this book was written to help couples that to move well beyond mutual misunderstandings. My hope is for reaching towards intimate connection and attempting to get to know each other more at each stage of the relationship, while still maintaining a sense of self. Making modern marriages work will require more than linear thinking.

Currently, relationships are seen as linear, for the most part. You meet, you commit, you do societal norms, you get older, you die. This model correlates quite well with the idea of mutual misunderstandings. You agree to disagree and all that. You take the good with the bad. But what if we could look at relationships as being much more multi-dimensional? What if two people could stretch beyond the continuum into many realms of life and still remain happily together? Conscious Curiosity aimed to look at the possibility of multi-dimensional relationships through the idea of leaving no stone unturned.

The relationships that I have learned from, inform what I know about how to nurture relationships — my parents have been and continue to be a great influence in my life. By telling you about them, more specifically my family background, you will understand better where I come from. Here is what I can offer, my family background and by default my story.

My parents celebrated their 50$^{th}$ Wedding Anniversary and both sets of my grandparents also celebrated over 50 years of marriage! Each of these events and the celebrations of lives lived together left lasting impressions on me about marriage and commitment to a life-long partner.

Marriage, as an institution, lives strong in my family. My brother and his wife have been married 20 years. My sister has been married 10 years. My husbands' brothers are both married longer than 7 years each. I have been married almost 23 years. The pressure to make relationships survive and thrive prevails in our families.

> Yes, I feel intense familial pressure to make my relationship thrive! I do not always cherish the pressure.

However, I find it difficult and challenging to be expected to live within the societal prescribed norms of marriage. I have had to continually figure out how to make being in a committed relationship work for me.

When I was less than six months married to my husband, I moved to a different state, without my husband, to start us (more like *Me*, you might think) on a "new journey." Clearly, we communicated and worked things out together and learned to stay together. Amazing because, we did not own cell phones at the time! Certainly, there is much more to this story. Also, it was not the only time we have been apart and together in our relationship. Sometimes moves happen for one person in a relationship and the other person follows up behind. But for now, back to the story of the huge doses of familial pressure to fit into current prescribed norms.

Most of my aunts and uncles have remained married to the same spouse. Natural to life, there have been a few bleeps here and there, and as of today in December of 2014, they are all married. Yes, out of 8 aunts and uncles, 4 relationships, they are all in committed marriages. I have 12 cousins from these aunts and uncles. Most of them are married or engaged and most have children as well. Gosh, yes my family is ultra-traditional.

Crazy, how can I pretend to be able to help others who are building their own type of family? Well, I am not pretending. I am writing from what I know, from my heart, and from compassion. I am aware that most family stories and connections through relationships are possibly richer and certainly more complicated than mine!

Our families might look all neat and tidy from the outside, but we all know that in life outward appearances are not everything. There are families with much more complex structures on the outside, that might be having an easier time behind closed doors. I will never know for sure.

I am not here to judge or evaluate other relationships and family structures. With all sincerity, all relationships are exactly as they should be. Each moment in time teaches. Being present and aware of exactly where you are in your relationship takes practice and patience. There is always room for change, improvement, and deeper understanding. The fact that my family is so darn "White Bread," well...as I said before, please don't think of us as being the "right" way or the "best" way to thrive. You being fully present to who you are and to whom you love is what is most important.

### A Bigger Dinner Table

I travelled in June of 2014 to celebrate my parents' 50th Wedding Anniversary. The event lasted several days, culminating in a boat party of 50 people honoring their marriage on a trip around the Statue of Liberty.

### Statue of Liberty

Both of my grandmothers arrived into the United States through the Statue of Liberty and Ellis Island checkpoint in their early teens. Adding up all the married years in my family, collectively, in three generations we have over 250 years of knowledge on how to create sustained relationships. I have not counted the relationships in my husbands' family! They are also kind of "white bread," so I find no need to give further details here.

The 250 years of marriage are not mine. I do not own 250 years of marriage advice. The years are collectively a part of my story and my history. Yet, I accept that I am not an expert. At the same time, I honor my ancestors. I come from who I am. Yet, I have not lived in their relationships. I have only lived in mine. Still, I do believe that some of their knowledge and who they were as people shines through in how I live my life. And, honestly 250 years is pretty impressive!

I pretended, while I wrote Conscious Curiosity that all sorts of great information from my ancestors magically flowed through my soul, brain and heart, and onto these pages!

While writing, June 2014 became my deadline, because what better time to present information on sustaining lasting relationships than at a family gathering for a long-lasting relationship. Also, the book is in many ways a tribute to my parents. I owe so much of who I am, how I operate in the world, and my values to their example of a sustained relationship to each other and to how they support our extended family. I went past my deadline; because books are harder to write than I thought! But I did finish! Now the content is ready for an even *bigger* dinner table, including yours!

I will end with a question. Are you willing to keep asking more questions to sustain the conversations you began? Are you willing to keep being continuously consciously curious?

If you are, then by all means put down this book and enjoy the life you have created. And thank you for joining me on this journey.

## Author's Notes

> Marry a man/woman you love to talk to. As you get older, their conversational skills will be as important as any other.
> — Unknown

### About the Original Title

Oh, yes, let's clarify the original title of this little book. SMD_LMP is an acronym for Suck My Dick and Lick My Pussy. Possibly you may have never picked up the book if I had kept the title as it was. Possibly you are one of those people who wishes I *had* kept the title as SMD_LMP. Either way, it is the same book, with countless changes here and there to make the new title stick — yet the content itself remained the same.

SMD_LMP is an in your face activity! Simple as that! Being present in each moment.

But I wonder, are you like I was a year ago? Maybe you don't or didn't know that SMD is a common short texting code for Suck My Dick. I am fortunate to have teenagers that are constantly teaching me new things! Being a parent of teens is a wonderful curious thing, you think you're smart and full of wisdom, but they teach you that you have more to learn. I am glad for this.

I tried to make up acronyms of my own. I added LMP, because communication is a two-way street — communication takes both people making an effort. This idea falls flat. The image if oral sex is all that comes to mind with SMD!

Like I said before, SMD_LMP is an in your face activity! Simple as that! And this book has content that is much more complex.

In the beginning, I developed the unfamiliar phrase in the form of an acronym as a continual reminder to myself to push beyond my boundaries, and take a leap into the unknown. I knew I would be sharing ideas I have about conversations and building committed relationships in an "In Your Face" kind of way.

SMD_LMP, now called Conscious Curiosity, is a book written and designed for couples. As you can clearly tell, this book, (whatever you title it: SMD_LMP or Conscious Curiosity) is not a sex manual, not now, nor will it ever be one. Ever. There is no pornographic material in this book.

But for now, let me explain why I almost kept the title that began as a moment in my life when I learned a little extra about embracing conversations and continuing communication — even when I wanted to run out on my relationships with the people I love.

The content in SMD_LMP, now Conscious Curiosity, relates to the give and take necessary to sustain lasting relationships. Let me phrase my idea bluntly, the only way to sustain a beautiful conversation is to give the other person your 100% undivided attention, very much as you would need to do if you were performing oral sex. Yes, I did say that, because good deep penetrating and fun conversations are really intense. So, ok be intense! Be consciously curious!

SMD_LMP (Conscious Curiosity) is also about the duality of relationships — the idea that there is a quality in things and ideas being two sided or of two parts. Coins are two sided, and as we all know, a one sided coin is a novelty and a two-sided coin has real value. Two-ply toilet paper is also made up of two parts. You can buy single-ply toilet paper but the good stuff is made of two parts! OK, so yea I had all sorts of good reasons for the original title — and then I changed the title to Conscious Curiosity.

Taken literally, the act of SMD_LMP cannot happen without the member and the lips. Both people need to be willing to give and take, listen and talk, and exchange these roles with fluidity. In conversation, people need to use both their mouth and their body to talk and their ears and eyes to listen.

> In conversation, when someone is talking, the other person needs to be listening and enjoying the moment of attempting to better understand his or her partner.

True communication and the act of sucking dick or licking pussy have one important thing in common: you cannot talk when you are giving the other person exactly what they really need!

Listen, in reality, SMD_LPM is a current day made up an acronym. Suck My Dick and Lick My Pussy are simply words strung together that form an image in the readers mind. Sure, words can be controversial if you let them be, or the ideas that words conjure up can be fodder for thought if you desire. What is it about the act of doing the activity of oral sex that brings pleasure? How can the pleasure of sex be brought to the sometimes mundane, yet vitally important, act of conversation? Why is it that a controversial title might have made a huge segment of the population not read the book at all?

> A bit of background, saying SMD_LMP is really hard for me! Actually, nearly impossible! Ask me the title of my book and you will see me gulp and hesitate. I'll smile and look uncomfortable in my body. Then I'll say the title and tiny miracles happen! Most people did not seem nearly as uncomfortable as I was when they heard me saying SMD_LMP, although, some were. And other people might have been being polite and I missed the cues, LOLs, but in the end I wrote the book and I have learned how to stand up and say my words. Then, after I said them out loud to over a hundred people, I changed the title…because I could.

I implore you to learn to be present, in the moment and intensely conscious of your preconceived thoughts, emotions, ideas, and relationship history. Find the curiosity of a child within you, and use that gift to become closer and more connected to your significant other. Use your curiosity to create room to be more open-minded.

Is it wrong to consider consciously curious conversation as being intensely intimate? I think not. We bring context to words in how we use them. We make meaning and create understanding through stories. SMD_LMP is a make-believe acronym about a penis and a pussy, nothing else! This book proposes that the ideas presented go beyond penises and pussies and considers the possibility of deep, penetrating, thought provoking, fascinating, interesting, and lasting conversations. And of course, another way to say this is to say that to love your partner you need a lifetime of conscious curiosity.

After all, because you are in a committed relationship, you will be talking to this person every day of your life for the rest of your life. Talking and listening are ways of feeling connected to your partner. Vital, loving communication with the intent towards understanding is more important than physical intimacy because conversations are a part of every day growth and development of a relationship. All of this technical stuff becomes easier to understand if you remember that to be curious about what makes the person you love feel happy is a recipe for success.

Do you need more convincing about why an in-your-face book on communication might be of some use to you? I ask you, what good is there in maintaining your status quo? Is your relationship and the connection to your partner really where you want it to be? Do you trust your significant other as much as you'd like to? Do you run into the same ol' same ol' stuff in your conversations? What good are these conversations that repeat themselves? What do you add to your life with your loved one when you begin to think to yourself, "crap, not this topic again!" I am asking you, "Do ya wanna grow?" Then, Ya gotta do something, anything new. You gotta try something hard to do.

Something hard to do is having the courage and faith to initiate crucial conversations and remain consciously curious. I am certain that you are aware, deep inside of you, of conversations that you have been avoiding. Try having at least one crucial conversation with your partner before you give up on this book or on each other.

I ask you to go have that crucial conversation. You know what it is, step out of the recesses of your mind, and be real in real time, and in real life with your partner. Be consciously curious.

I wrote this book for adults, but originally I had a title more suited to teens who text and use slang. Slang exists. Being uncomfortable with the words we have to choose from to communicate also exists. Forms of communication are constantly changing — and so should you.

plmk

Once you have read and used the book, plmk (please let me know) how I could have made it better. Please also let me and others know what worked for you. I am easy to approach, find me on Facebook, Pinterest, Linkedin, Instagram, Twitter, and basically all over the internet, best of all you can find me through my website at www.SuzanneGibbs.com. Thanks, and plmk what you think.

# Acknowledgements

> Whenever I want to laugh, I read a wonderful book, 'Children's Letters to God.' You can open it anywhere. One I read recently said, "Dear God, thank you for the baby brother, but what I prayed for was a puppy." — Maya Angelou

## To My Husband

A thank you, a hug, and a kiss go to my husband, Derek, who believes in me, even when I falter. I love you. I also am thankful for the countless hours of talking and listening you endured while I wrote this book and perfected my vision for what I desired to bring to others by running my ideas through you. You're a champ!

## To My Children

I need to take a moment to give credit were credit is due. Commitment, like SMD_LMP or Conscious Curiosity is a two-way street. I took the unused title SMD_LMP from my teenaged boys because they gave me permission to use their words. They made me promise that I would give credit to them for using their words. They don't own the words, but they did introduce me to the many varied uses of SMD. So, I say to you both:

Thank You for teaching me so much about listening, talking, and being open to unusual twists and turns in conversation. Thank you for ALWAYS being willing to say what it is that you want to say, even when you knew I did not want to hear the words! I thank you for the lessons you never knew you were teaching me in language usage, twists and turns in conversation, and risky sarcasm. You have taught me so much!

Thank you for asking me to not yell at you as I was raising you. Through not yelling I learned that it was me that needed a time out. Thank you for being brave enough to tell me what you really think and saw as truths in our family through your eyes. Wow, some of the information you shared hurt, and was hard to process. Thank you also for teaching me how to create texts in shorthand and use acronyms. Thank you for all your unsolicited feedback on this book while I typed away every day for months on end. The book would have been a weaker book without you, and in many ways, not even possible at all. Learning some of the language of your generation made ideas in the stories in this book possible. Yes, you can still use slang in our house, all I ask is please don't stop talking to me. And, SMD_LMP boys, because whether you meant to or not, you taught your old Mom a trick or two! Colby and Jeffrey, you guys are the best!

**To My Sister**

I am grateful to my sister Samantha for her endless hours of editing. The book became much more polished and fluid under her "eagle eye." Thank you so much also for not ridiculing my idea about writing a book comparing oral sex to conversation, I was so afraid to tell you about it early on in its creation, but I knew I needed your help.

**To My Friends from Long Beach**

No words can express the gratitude I have for your unwavering support. I am tickled that you all were the first to hear excerpts from my unfinished book read out loud to you, by me. Your feedback and encouragement gave me so much hope that I would indeed finish this project and that it would reach others in ways as yet unknown to me. I adored your vision of me in the future talking to Katie Couric on the Today Show and Oprah on her show. I never imagined going to such a large audience, but then with your support, why not? Thank you from the bottom of my creative spirit. I hope I can make good on your vision for me, and for the book, but most of all for all couples in need of a bit of Conscious Curiosity to intensify their relationship!

**To My BETA Readers and Helpers from Around the World**

I am forever indebted to each of you. For wanting to read this whole book before it was published and give me feedback to make an improved impression for a larger audience. Each of you gave the book insight that I could never have had without your help. Also, thank you for continually asking me, "How's it going?" And keeping me working on a project that at times felt too big and daunting. I am ever so grateful. To each of you, and you know who you are, that I relied on for guidance, support, technical questions, and a listening ear — who would have known I'd need such a large community to bring a project to life! To my social media friends far and wide, for commenting, supporting and making me feel less alone as I wrote and wrote — thank you.

**To You, The Reader**

Dear reader, I hope you have enjoyed this book about both sides of a committed relationship — the serious work of making it real and the fun and joy of life together. SMD_LMP requires give and take and the duality of two parties — YOU — working together, and so does believing in Conscious Curiosity. Go for it! Keep it up, and thanks so much for reading.

## Resources List

This is not your typical resources list. I have compiled books here that I have read and that have served to inspire me to keep my creative embers flowing and thus to have the courage to write this book. Many of the books I list have absolutely nothing to do with creating conversation in relationships or in remaining consciously curious. This resources list is by no means exhaustive. This list is in no particular order. I am an avid reader and could not include everything that has influenced me. Still, you might find inspiration here, I did!

The Artist's Way, Julia Cameron

An Unknown Woman, Alice Koller

I am Malala: The girl who stood up for education and was shot by the Taliban, Malala Yousafzai and Christina Lamb

The Signature of all Things, and Committed: A Love Story, and Eat, Pray, Love, Elizabeth Gilbert

Communication Miracles for Couples: Easy and Effective Tools to Create More Love and Less Conflict, Jonathan Robinson

The Proper Care and Feeding of Husbands, Dr. Laura Schlessinger (I cannot believe it but I am admitting that I have read this, twice!)

Hyperbole and a Half: Unfortunate Situations, Flawed Coping Mechanisms, Mayhem, and Other Things That Happened..., Allie Brosh

Books of Adam: The Blunder Years, Adam Ellis

Everyone Poops (My Body Science Series), Taro Gomi and Amanda Mayer Stinchecum

## Suzanne Gibbs

Harold and the Purple Crayon, Crockett Johnson (my absolute favorite book)

Steal Like an Artist, Austin Kleon

Writing Down the Bones: Freeing the Writer Within, Natalie Goldberg

This Is A Story of a Happy Marriage, Ann Patchett

Write It Down, Make It Happen: Knowing What You Want And Getting It, Anne Klauser

How Conversation Works: 6 Lessons for Better Communication, Anne Curzan

Painting The Walls Red: The Uninhibited Woman's Guide to a Fabulous Life After 40, Judy Ford

The Feminine Mystique, Betty Friedan

Lean In: Women, Work, and the Will to Lead, Sheryl Sandberg

A Room of One's Own, Virginia Woolf

Happier at Home and The Happiness Project, Gretchen Rubin

F**k It!: The Ultimate Spiritual Way, John C. Parkin

An Illustrated Life, Danny Gregory

The Artist's Guide: How to Make a Living Doing What You Love, Jackie Battenfield

Go the Fuck To Sleep, Adam Mansbach

Daring Greatly, Brene Brown

## About the Author

Suzanne Gibbs was born in Madison, WI where she lived for a few months. By age 49 she lived in 38 addresses including her formative years spent abroad in Mexico and Brazil.

Leaving beautiful Brazil for New Jersey as a teenager was confusing and upsetting. The American culture and words such as fair-isle, suburb, and blucher's were completely unknown and a great cause for upset. During this time Suzanne began practicing daily writing; this ritual continues to serve her creative process and informs her work.

In college, at Carnegie-Mellon University, she studied Graphic Design. She later enrolled at University of Portland (Oregon) in Communication Studies at the graduate level to more deeply hone her writing and communication skills.

Degrees aside, she took a leap into motherhood and enjoyed the life of stay-at-home parent. Her time at home allowed for continued interest in creative endeavors. In 2013 Suzanne graduated with a Master of Fine Art from Claremont Graduate University. Suzanne's thesis show titled, Three Squares A Day, was a visual amalgamation of her ideas about home craft and fine art. She questions: Why are home crafts less valuable than fine art works? How is value measured? Does a dollar amount amassed measure true value? Do history books measure value? She will always wonder.

In Suzanne's world, art making is critical to the construction of a well-lived life. Suzanne uses painting and drawing as her primary medium to communicate visually, her computer and words to communicate through stories. She shares her time and talents through lectures and workshops, participating on artist panels, and facilitating discussion groups about art, the creative process, and learning to see and understand through viewing art.

Suzanne publishes a blog called: Notes On Art: Interviews, Influences, and In The Studio. Conscious Curiosity is her first book.